FUKUSHIMA

311

Is the enduring aftermath of the Fukushima nuclear disaster killing off the Earth?

Col. Walter T. Richmond

New York
United States of America

DEDICATION

To the wonderful, strong, and brave people of Fukushima and Japan who simply want to get back to living happy healthy lives after twice suffering – first from the horrific tsunami *and then* the nuclear disaster that followed. Our thoughts and prayers are with you for a fast and healthy recovery wherever life finds you.

To the truth-seekers world-wide who simply want to be able to make decisions and take actions based on facts – facts devoid of media spin and official distortions. Without a clear lens, seeing the truth is impossible.

To the citizens, citizen-journalists, citizen-scientists, and others who continue to report and post what they see and hear happening regardless of the consequences – you have our admiration and deep respect.

◆————————————————————◆

This book is not anti-nuclear power or pro-nuclear power. It is pro-people and pro-truth. Without honest discourse, probing questions, and detailed investigations based on transparency and facts, we have nothing but agenda-driven propaganda which is the enemy of free expression and reality.

CONTENTS

ABOUT "WE"

Fukushima "311"
In Japan the tsunami and Fukushima nuclear disaster date of March 11, 2011, is often referred to as simply "311," akin to the way Americans might refer to the September 11, 2001 terror attacks as "911."

How "we" got here
"Col. Walter T. Richmond" is a pseudonym for our group of authors who recently joined together to write *Vikings Rising* and, before that, *Hasta la Vista Europe* where we exposed how various information being related by eye witnesses, statistics, and other on-the-ground sources seemed to be diametrically opposed to the versions the old-fashioned-controlled media was busily creating.

Since the keepers of the "approved politically correct version of events" try and spin "the story," marginalize the message, distract people with silliness, and anything else to misdirect the spotlight, we chose one of us to represent all of us – under our penname – in the spirit of freedom of the press and to "tell it like it is." The big story is about truths and not about us. In line with that, we wrote this final version with a one-author voice. And we again self-published to avoid editors and others who could potentially cut important sections or sugarcoat things to make them more palatable.

Writing style

Here we'll repeat our warning to readers of our last books – our writing style is rather conversational. Like a chat between friends. Maybe it's the way we feel most comfortable relaying information. And since we aren't compiling an academic tome or lofty work of research, you'll see that we shattered, trounced, and ignored a whole volume of "good grammar" rules and writing style guides in the last few sentences alone. Accept it. We'll be doing a lot more. And, when we start sentences with "and," and when we construct long sentences worthy of Tolstoy, or snippets worthy of social media mania, look past the words to get to the big picture.

Sources, citations, citings, and sightings

We felt it important to provide links to our sources to allow you to do your own research and form your own opinions. Of course, explore the links at your own risk and with caution since all links are third party sites and we can't and don't guarantee safety, appropriateness of content, or anything else related to those links. (We've also noticed web pages have been vanishing.)

Source checking *Then & Now*

As to the actual content we investigated, we tried to double and triple check stories and sources like the old fashioned journalists some of us still try to be.

These days, major media outlets seem to pump out content with little if any corroboration, as is witnessed by the bunk that regularly floods the presses. From imagined military escapades to pretend weapons of mass destruction, from self-drawn symbols of hatred to other preposterous claims, the old-fashioned-controlled media routinely blames its steady stream of snafus on a lack of time to check facts or on a lack of budget to hire fact checkers or whatever is convenient – which all adds up to a bunch of slick professional entertainers mindlessly reading teleprompters and rushing from deadline to deadline without having to think or analyze anything deeper than the next deadline. Although major media outlets seem to be encouraging more and more reporters to blurt out their "opinions," the opinions often sound scripted, and are quite often "textbook party line." Also, disturbingly, comment sections on main stream media sites are disappearing, closed, or heavily censored.

At times we've used italics to signify thoughts. Other times we've used italics to break up sections. And we may have also occasionally stressed poignant points within quotes by using italics to help us highlight them. We endeavored to ensure accuracy, but will not be held responsible for any errors, omissions, inaccuracies, et cetera. Regrettably mistakes happen.

The Golden Rule
Finally, we believe that every people on this Earth have a right to live free, in peace and harmony, in their own space, pursuing their own cultures, following whatever customs and traditions they fancy, so long as they harm none. To each his own. Live and let live. No hate. Just facts and figures and truths.

Do to others as you would have them do to you. Peace.

NUCLEAR POWER PLANT DISASTERS 101

Nuclear power plants are built to create electricity via nuclear reactions. Apart from highly specialized scientists and engineers, most people have no real grasp of the intricacies of nuclear power plant operations, nuclear reactions, and the potential for disaster.

Neither do we…

But here's a quick, and admittedly simplified, overview that may make the process easier to envision.[1]

1) Extreme heat and radiation is generated when a nuclear reaction occurs – uranium atoms are split inside of a reactor.
2) The heat is then used to turn water into steam.
3) The steam is used to turn a turbine
4) The spinning turbine cranks a generator to make electricity.
5) The used steam is then turned back into water by a condenser so that the resulting water is ready to be pumped back into the system when more steam is needed.

---

[1] environmentalscience.org/nuclear-energy

Some of the main things that can go wrong center around nuclear radiation and contamination from the improper storage and disposal of radioactive materials as well as "meltdown" events. Because of the extreme heat produced in the reactor, if it isn't cooled sufficiently, the fuel rods could melt and release radioactive fuel.[2] "In a worst-case meltdown scenario the puddle of hot fuel could melt through the steel containment vessel and through subsequent barriers meant to contain the nuclear material, exposing massive quantities of radioactivity to the outside world."[3]

So if a nuclear power plant loses power, and can no longer cool its super-hot nuclear fuel rods, because, for instance, a tsunami knocks out its electricity, well then there exists the very serious risk of a meltdown event...

And after a meltdown that releases radioactivity, tracking that emission is done by identifying the specific radioisotope (radioactive isotopes) that the disaster released. "Fukushima's signature radioisotopes (are) cesium-134 and cesium-137."[4]

If you find cesium-134 and/or cesium-137 in a sample you're testing... the Fukushima alarm bell should go off.

Now we go back to 1896...

---

[2] scientificamerican.com/article/nuclear-energy-primer/

[3] scientificamerican.com/article/nuclear-energy-primer/

[4] patch.com/california/paloalto/stanford-uses-fukushima-radiation-to-track-tuna

FOREWORD
JUNE 15, 1896

"Victims were found with fractured skulls, broken legs,
or without arms."

*— Part of the inscription on the Monument in Ryouri,
Japan honoring victims of the 1896 Meiji Sanriku tsunami
disaster*

June 15, 1896 was a day of great celebration in the towns and communities on the Sanriku coast of Japan.[5]

The traditional Shinto "Boy's Festival" honoring boys – with families praying for the "health, happiness, and prosperity of boys, and to protect them from evil spirits"[6] was in full swing. Additionally, festivities for returning soldiers from the Sino-Japanese War were also underway. After fighting for influence in Korea, Japan had scored a huge victory over China and had dealt the far-larger but poorly organized Chinese a major military blow.

Against this backdrop of merriment, joy, and pride, who could have predicted the carnage that was about to claim

---

[5] shippai.org/fkd/en/cfen/CA1000616.html

[6] wheeloftheyear.com/2018/taoist&shinto.htm

more than 4 times the number of soldiers killed in the Sino-Japanese War in the span of mere moments?

Hints of impending doom

Few villagers had paid much attention to some recent strange anomalies. Wells that had suddenly dried up or had very low levels were noted with curiosity but not much concern. Large daily tuna catches as well as a huge sardine school swimming near the coast certainly didn't seem ominous either – and neither were the many little earthquake shocks experienced by the coastal villages over the past months.

At around 7:30 pm, as families were having dinner, many felt a minor underground shock. It would be later learned that an 8.5 magnitude earthquake had occurred about 100 miles off the coast.

Some 30 minutes later, it is said that local fishermen heard a sound like distant thunder as they noticed the tide quickly recede exposing undersea land…

Tsunami rising

The first devastating tsunami wave smashed into the shoreline around 8:07 pm followed within minutes by a second tsunami wave. The "highest wave reached an incredible height of 38.2 meters" (just over 125 feet).[7] The tsunami claimed almost 9,000 homes and more than 22,000 lives as the shores of Sanriku were mercilessly pummeled.

---

[7] shippai.org/fkd/en/cfen/CA1000616.html

In September 1896, writing for the National Geographic, Eliza Ruhamah Scidmore reported about the tsunami noting that "a few survivors, who saw it advancing in the darkness, report its height at 80-100 feet."[8] Stating that the waves had "stranded" about 300 large nautical vessels and had destroyed or swept away "10,000 fishing boats," Scidmore described how rescue efforts and help were initially slow to arrive to the remote areas because "telegraph offices, instruments, and operators" had been "carried away."[9] In Japanese seismic history, it was one of the most destructive disasters.

Historically speaking, though, it was par for the course...

Records show that tsunamis have been wreaking havoc along the Sanriku coastline since at least 500 BC.[10]

Far more recently, in 1933, another in a long string of these earthquake/tsunami incidents in the region created a 90+ foot wave that wiped out 7,000 homes while leaving thousands dead or missing and 12,053 injured.[11]

With a long history of tsunamis, this sounds like a great place to locate a nuclear reactor, right?

Why, yes... exactly...

---

[8] archive.org/details/nationalgeograph71896nati/page/n479

[9] archive.org/details/nationalgeograph71896nati/page/286

[10] jishin.go.jp/main/chousakenkyuu/miyagi_juten/h18/h18_miyagi.pdf

[11] Corkill, Edan, "Heights of survival", Japan Times, 12 June 2011, pp. 9–10

Fateful decisions

It was in this tsunami-prone region that TEPCO (Tokyo Electric Power Company) decided to locate a nuclear power plant... Worse, while seeking government permission to construct their nuclear power plant in the 1960s, TEPCO stated in their application that "In the past 700 years, Fukushima suffered almost no noteworthy damage from earthquakes except in the Aizu area (in current Fukushima Prefecture)."[12]

The danger from tsunamis was not properly addressed.

Throwing historical records to the wind, "in designing the Fukushima No. 1 plant in the 1960s, TEPCO estimated the maximum possible tsunami would be only up to 3.1 meters... In 2002, however, following recommendations from quake experts at the Japan Society of Civil Engineering, TEPCO modified the facilities, so they could withstand a tsunami of up to 5.7 meters (18.7 feet). This was also approved by the regulators..."[13]

So TEPCO was ready for a maximum of about a 19 foot tsunami wave... If you didn't just twinge, re-read the wave heights of the killer tsunamis that occurred not so terribly long ago in 1896 and 1933...

And worse, again, it seems that the decision to build the nuclear plant low and close to the ocean was, in part, a function of... *wait for it...* profit.

---

[12] japantimes.co.jp/news/2011/07/13/national/fukushima-plant-site-originally-was-a-hill-safe-from-tsunami/

[13] japantimes.co.jp/news/2011/07/13/national/fukushima-plant-site-originally-was-a-hill-safe-from-tsunami

Japan Times revealed in 2011 that, "in fact, TEPCO decided to build the plant on low ground based on a cost-benefit calculation of the operating costs of the seawater pumps, according to two research papers separately written by senior TEPCO engineers in the 1960s... If the seawater pumps were placed on high ground, their operating costs would be accordingly higher..."[14]

Seriously. It really was all a matter of saving cash and according to TEPCO, "'We decided to build the plant at ground level after comparing the ground construction costs and operating costs of the circulation water pumps,' wrote...deputy head of the TEPCO's construction office at the Fukushima No. 1 plant..."[15]

So instead of building on a 115-foot-high hill near the Pacific, "TEPCO, assuming tsunamis 3.1 meters (10.2 feet) or higher would never hit the coast, reduced the (hill) by some 25 meters (82 fcct) and erected the plant on artificially prepared ground only 10 meters (32.8 feet) above sea level..."[16] By **REDUCING THE HILL**, TEPCO put the nuclear plant firmly on solid bedrock, but woefully low. *Russian-roulette low...*

The first nuclear plant came online in 1970.

A tsunami-proven region. Low height construction. Proximity to the ocean to save cash – the eventual catastrophe seems quite predictable...

---

[14] japantimes.co.jp/news/2011/07/13/national/fukushima-plant-site-originally-was-a-hill-safe-from-tsunami

[15] japantimes.co.jp/news/2011/07/13/national/fukushima-plant-site-originally-was-a-hill-safe-from-tsunami

[16]16 japantimes.co.jp/news/2011/07/13/national/fukushima-plant-site-originally-was-a-hill-safe-from-tsunami

SEPTEMBER 2, 2002

"What happened in Japan is terrible, and there are many reasons it should have been avoided."

— Bill Gates[17]

TEPCO's Chairman, President, Vice President, and several advisers all announced their resignations in 2002 after it was revealed that TEPCO "may have failed to accurately report cracks at its nuclear reactors in the late 1980s and 1990s... The company and the Japanese government are probing whether workers covered up reports of the cracks...TEPCO is suspected of falsifying 29 cases of safety repair records..."[18]

"'There is no room for excuses,' TEPCO President Nobuya Minami said... as he announced he would leave his post in mid-October... 'I deeply regret the incident and cannot apologize enough for it.'"[19]

Just you wait...

---

[17] wired.com/2011/06/mf-qagates/

[18] web.archive.org/web/20110315065851/http://archives.cnn.com/2002/BUSINESS/asia/09/02/japan.tepco/index.html

[19] web.archive.org/web/20110315065851/http://archives.cnn.com/2002/BUSINESS/asia/09/02/japan.tepco/index.html

In prior years, TEPCO had a number of other problems with the Fukushima Daiichi Plant including falling fuel rods,[20] a high-pressure alarm manual shutdown,[21] over-insertion of control blades,[22] and an automatic SCRAM – an emergency shutdown due to low water levels.[23]

Tick, tick, tick...

---

[20] wsj.com/articles/SB10001424052748704396504576204461929992144

[21] tepco.co.jp/cc/press/09022501-j.html

[22] tepco.co.jp/cc/press/09032602-j.html

[23] tepco.co.jp/cc/press/10110201-j.html

MARCH 7, 2011

"We're in a giant car heading towards a brick wall and everyone's arguing over where they're going to sit!"

— David Suzuki[24]

TEPCO submitted a report to let Japan's Nuclear Safety Agency know that TEPCO had "predicted in 2008 that a tsunami over 10 meters (32.8 feet) high could hit the plant, which was only designed to withstand tsunami of 5.7 meters (18.7 feet)... TEPCO had predicted that waves between 8.4 and 10.2 meters (27.6 – 33.5 feet) high could hit all 6 reactors at the plant in the event of an earthquake similar to one that devastated the area in 1896..."[25]

"In the report, TEPCO also said it would begin examining the plant's tsunami-resistance measures... (and) planned to deal appropriately with the matter by around October of 2012..."[26]

A little too little... a little too late...

---

[24] suzukidavid.weebly.com/

[25] web.archive.org/web/20111028152753/http://www.jaif.or.jp/english/news_images/pdf/ENGNEWS01_1317702304P.pdf

[26] web.archive.org/web/20111028152753/http://www.jaif.or.jp/english/news_images/pdf/ENGNEWS01_1317702304P.pdf

MARCH 11, 2011

"The Japanese identity is one of selfishness. We need to use the tsunami to wash away this selfishness. I think it's God's punishment."

— Tokyo Governor Shintaro Ishihara[27]

Japan sits "atop four huge slabs of the Earth's crust, called tectonic plates. These plates mash and grind together and trigger... earthquakes." Thus, Japan experiences around 1,500 earthquakes annually and minor daily tremors are routine.[28] You get used to it.

Fukushima is the name of the 3rd largest prefecture (like a "state") in the Northeast region of Japan. Its capital is the city of Fukushima, one of many towns and cities that make up that prefecture. The actual initial nuclear plant disaster happened in Ōkuma, on the Pacific coast in the Fukushima prefecture.

March 11, 2011 was by all accounts a normal sunny day in Fukushima, a little windy and maybe a bit chilly, with temperatures averaging about 33°F. There had been some large foreshocks felt in Fukushima, but nothing

---

[27] japantimes.co.jp/community/2011/12/27/general/2011-a-year-of-disaster-in-quotes

[28] livescience.com/30312-japan-earthquakes-top-10-110408.html

seemed terribly out of sorts. Minor earthquakes and trembles are pretty common in the area.

One of the biggest

Then around 2:46 pm, a 9.1 magnitude underwater earthquake rocked both the seabed and coast about 45 miles east of Japan's coastline.[29] It shook for about 6 long minutes.[30] Called the Tohoku Earthquake, it became the 4th largest recorded earthquake in the world according to the USGS (United States Geological Survey).[31] After the main earthquake, hundreds of aftershocks followed.

Tsunami rising… again

Within an hour, the tsunamis that followed devastated the coastline and "waves reached run-up heights (how far the wave surges inland above sea level) of up to 128 feet (39 meters) at Miyako city and traveled inland as far as 6 miles (10 km) in Sendai. The tsunami flooded an estimated area of approximately 217 square miles (561 square kilometers) in Japan."[32]

According to the New York Times, "The 2011 disaster killed almost 16,000 people as sea waves rose as high as 130 feet… An additional 2,500 were reported missing and never found."[33]

Utter devastation. Possibly only a nuclear disaster could make things worse…

---

[29] earthquake.usgs.gov/earthquakes/eventpage/official20110311054624120_30

[30] livescience.com/39110-japan-2011-earthquake-tsunami-facts.html

[31] earthquake.usgs.gov/earthquakes/browse/largest-world.php

[32] livescience.com/39110-japan-2011-earthquake-tsunami-facts.html

[33] nytimes.com/2016/11/21/world/asia/japan-earthquake.html

The UK Telegraph reported that around 3:46 pm, a large 46+ foot tsunami wave easily went over the Fukushima Daiichi Plant "seawall" which was designed to stop waves up to only 19 feet high... TEPCO officials told the media that "the plant was designed to be resistant to an 18 foot wave but was struck by a wall of water more than 22 feet in height."[34] ("More than 22 feet" in TEPCO-speak seems to mean 46+ feet...)

More recently, according to the World Nuclear Association in a report updated in June 2018, "Following a major earthquake, a 15-metre (49.2 foot) tsunami disabled the power supply and cooling of three Fukushima Daiichi reactors, causing a nuclear accident on 11 March 2011. All three cores largely melted in the first three days."[35]

Initially, the world's focus was on the endless videos of tsunami-carnage, as deadly walls of water swept away people, towns, cars, buildings, boats, trucks – just about everything in its path.

Amidst the horrors of that day, Japan declared a state of emergency, started to help survivors and tried to figure out how to clean up from the tsunami devastation. TEPCO desperately attempted to respond to an increasingly overwhelming radioactive disaster.

Things didn't go well...

---

[34] telegraph.co.uk/news/worldnews/asia/japan/8392730/Japan-nuclear-crisis-tsunami-study-showed-Fukushima-plant-was-at-risk.html
[35] world-nuclear.org/information-library/safety-and-security/safety-of-plants/fukushima-accident.aspx

RADIOACTIVE FAILURES

"More than 30 of America's 100 nuclear power reactors have the same brand of General Electric reactors or containment system used in Fukushima."

— Bill Dedman

As the world watched things go from bad to worse, it became increasingly clear that the Fukushima nuclear facility was in big trouble.

The Japanese government declared a nuclear emergency during the mid-morning of March 11, 2011[36] and then issued evacuation orders for anyone within 3 km. People living beyond 3 km were advised "there is no danger and to carry on with their normal activities."[37]

Stay indoors

So initially, residents within 3 km of the Fukushima nuclear plants were ordered to evacuate. People 3 km-10 km away were told to stay home[38] since according to a government spokesperson "It's possible that

---

[36] telegraph.co.uk/news/worldnews/asia/japan/8383473/Japan-nuclear-crisis-Timeline-of-official-statements.html

[37] telegraph.co.uk/news/worldnews/asia/japan/8383473/Japan-nuclear-crisis-Timeline-of-official-statements.html

[38] bbc.com/news/science-environment-12722719

radioactive material in the reactor vessel could leak outside but the amount is expected to be small and the wind blowing towards the sea will be considerable."[39]

No danger
The evening of March 11, 2011, with dangerous pressure building up in one of the Fukushima reactors, nuclear plant engineers decided to relieve the stress by venting steam... thereby releasing radioactive material into the atmosphere. TEPCO said there was no danger.[40]

Definitely no danger
Early in the morning of March 12, 2011, the Chief Cabinet Secretary of Japan reassured everyone that "We are not in a situation in which residents face health damage."[41]

Ka-boom
Later that day, a violent explosion at the facility blew an enormous billowing cloud of radioactive dust into the sky.[42]

Stay indoors
On March 12, 2011, evacuation orders were issued to include everyone within 20 km of the nuclear power facility. Residents between 20 km and 30 km away were ordered to *stay indoors...*[43]

---

[39] telegraph.co.uk/news/worldnews/asia/japan/8383473/Japan-nuclear-crisis-Timeline-of-official-statements.html

[40] telegraph.co.uk/news/worldnews/asia/japan/8383473/Japan-nuclear-crisis-Timeline-of-official-statements.html

[41] pri.org/stories/2011-03-12/explosion-japans-quake-hit-nuclear-plant-video

[42] youtu.be/BdbitRlbLDc

[43] bbc.com/news/science-environment-12722719

Radiation levels "dropping"

Also on March 12, 2011, the Japanese government announced good news – "radiation emanating from the plant appeared to have decreased after Saturday's blast there, which produced a cloud of white smoke that obscured the complex."[44]

How the radiation level mysteriously dropped wasn't addressed...

"Safe" radiation levels

By March 13, 2011, Japan's Chief Cabinet Secretary was again reassuring everybody that although TEPCO was actively venting more steam out of the reactors and using seawater to try and cool off the reactors, that the "radiation released in the process is low enough not to affect people's health."[45]

On March 13 and 14, 2011, the Chief Cabinet Secretary warned that another explosion was *possible* but that "If there is an explosion, however, there would be no significant impact on human health."[46]

Ka-boom but no "harmful levels" of radiation

By the end of the day on March 14, 2011, the expected explosion happened and spewed radioactive clouds of material into the sky. The same day, authorities admitted all three reactors were apparently having dreaded fuel rod meltdowns, but a Japanese cabinet

---

[44] cbsnews.com/news/japans-chernobyl-quake-sparks-meltdown-fears/
[45] articles.latimes.com/2011/mar/12/world/la-fgw-japan-quake-reactor
[46] huffingtonpost.com/2011/03/13/japan-onagawa-nuclear-plant-state-of-emergency_n_835059.html

official reassured everyone that, "We have no evidence of harmful radiation exposure."[47]

If you're getting frustrated as a reader by all these mixed messages, imagine what it must have felt like to be living near Fukushima at that time...

No more sugar-coating

On March 15, 2011, with a fourth reactor on fire and following a third explosion, CBS-WJZ reported that Japan's Prime Minister now was warning that "The level seems very high and there is still a very high risk of more radiation coming out."[48] More people were actively evacuated.

Actually, now it's bad

The Chief Cabinet Secretary warned that "now we are talking about levels that can damage human health. These are readings taken near the area where we believe the releases are happening. Far away, the levels should be lower... Please do not go outside. Please stay indoors. Please close windows and make your homes airtight. Don't turn on ventilators. Please hang your laundry indoors."[49]

Limited access to info?

On March 16, 2011, US Ambassador-to-Japan Roos issued an official statement in which he said that US nuclear experts had been working "around the clock" to

---

[47] newyorker.com/news/news-desk/the-crisis-in-a-nutshell-the-danger-of-a-radioactive-cloud

[48] archive.org/details/WJZ_20110315_100000_Eyewitness_News_Morning_Edition/start/120/end/180

[49] csmonitor.com/World/Global-News/2011/0315/Japan-officials-Stay-indoors-nuclear-leaks-now-dangerous

analyze radiation dangers but "at times we have had only limited access to information…"[50]

Limited access at a time like this? Seriously??

Sure enough, among other data "limitations," information on "the movement of the radioactive plume and the information in the radiation dose based on SPEEDI (System for Prediction of Environmental Emergency Dose Information) was not released immediately…"[51]

US Ambassador Roos also stated that "After a careful analysis of data, radiation levels, and damage assessments of all units at Fukushima, our experts are in agreement with the response and measures taken by Japanese technicians, including their recommended 20 km radius for evacuation and additional shelter-in-place recommendations out to 30 km."[52]

So the US officially agreed that the Japanese should evacuate anyone within the 20 km radius… Ok.

Which makes the next directive that much more curious…

Americans should keep 400% further away…
On that same day, March 16, 2011, the United States Government issued a warning to **US citizens in Japan** to stay *at least* 80 km away from the Fukushima nuclear

---

[50] diplopundit.net/2011/03/15/us-ambassador-roos-issues-statement-on-japans-ongoing-nuclear-emergency/

[51] fukushimaontheglobe.com/the-earthquake-and-the-nuclear-accident/whats-happened

[52] diplopundit.net/2011/03/15/us-ambassador-roos-issues-statement-on-japans-ongoing-nuclear-emergency/

facilities, and if evacuation wasn't safe or practical, then "'to take shelter indoors'... The U.S. Embassy in Tokyo issued the advice in a statement distributed to reporters accompanying Secretary of State Hillary Clinton on a trip to Egypt..."[53]

Weird. On one hand we officially agree with a 20 km evacuation radius for Japanese citizens, but tell our own citizens living in Japan to stay 80 km away...

Circles and bigger circles
The crazier thing was that all the official Japanese evacuation orders seem to have been based on circles drawn around the disaster site – and not on actual radiation levels – yielding predictable results. "The contamination greatly differs based on the direction of the wind and the terrain rather than spreading concentrically. There were quite a few people who were evacuated to areas which were more contaminated than their original place as a result of following the government's evacuation order."[54]

Clearly, with radioactive material being moved around by rain and wind, circles and graphs didn't tell the whole story.

In just one telling example, "many people did not know that the wind and the rain on March 15th spread radioactive particles in a northwest direction from the NPP (Nuclear Power Plant)." Had they been told, maybe some would have stayed indoors...

---

[53] reuters.com/article/us-japan-usa-shelter-idUSTRE72F73J20110316

[54] fukushimaontheglobe.com/the-earthquake-and-the-nuclear-accident/whats-happened

Without continuously measuring actual radiation levels, and *making that information public,* how could anyone be expected to make smart evacuation decisions?

But mass evacuate they did.

About 160,000 people left, some inadvertently taking radioactive material along with them on their shoes, clothes, cars, luggage, pets, whatever...

Months later, same problems

The Economist reported on October 8, 2011, that a village 45 km away from Fukushima was discovered to have very high radiation levels. 45 km is 15 km further away than mandated, yet reportedly, wind gusts would shake "invisible particles of radioactive cesium off the trees and showers them over the village. Radiation levels in the hills are so high that villagers dare not go near them."[55] But because of circles drawn on maps instead of decisions based on radiation-level-readings, stories such as this one weren't rare.

Temporary housing

In the meanwhile, tens of thousands of people were fleeing the area with nowhere to go... Therefore, many were placed in temporary housing described by a US documentary filmmaker as "quite unpleasant." Why? "The houses are very small, you can hear people through the walls, you can hear people flushing the toilet three or four floors down. In the places where the communities are not very strong, there is still a lot of

---

[55] economist.com/asia/2011/10/08/hot-spots-and-blind-spots

animosity between neighbors, lots of people just stuck inside and never come out."

Imagine... you survive a tsunami disaster. Then you escape from a nuclear disaster. All to live in a shoebox for an undefined amount of time... Disheartening to say the least...

In an extraordinarily clear-cut observation, the US filmmaker added that he felt the "authorities in Japan want locals to think 'nothing happened.'"[56]

But happen it did.

By the way, in fairness to them, numerous outlets of the main stream media (MSM), and various reporters did and do cover the Fukushima disaster. But in today's culture of short messages and video snippets and even shorter attention spans, coupled with orchestrated distractions, obligatory selfies and food photos, *that's just not good enough.*

If you want to get through to your audience, these days, you need to repeat *and* repeat *and* repeat a message until it makes the desired impact. And in the case of Fukushima, it isn't happening, leaving most people with their heads in the clouds... *dangerous clouds.*

---

[56] rt.com/news/335219-deaths-fukushima-nuclear-jousan/

RADIOACTIVE CLOUD

"We should recognize from the start that just like Chernobyl, the Fukushima Daiichi plant has released radioactive materials equivalent in the amount to tens of nuclear bombs, and the resulting contamination is far worse than the contamination by a nuclear bomb."

— Tatsuhiko Kodama
Director of the Radioisotope Center
University of Tokyo[57]

Remember lying on your back as a kid watching the clouds float by? Imagining what shapes you could find? Like cesium-137? Glowing *from excitement?*

Nine days following the Fukushima event, a "radioactive cloud had crossed Northern America." A station in Iceland "picked up radioactive materials." Three days later "it was clear that the cloud had reached Europe."[58]

Within 15 days, radioactivity from Fukushima was "detectable all across the northern hemisphere. For the first four weeks, the radioactive materials remained confined to the northern hemisphere, with the equator

---

[57] japantimes.co.jp/community/2011/12/27/general/2011-a-year-of-disaster-in-quotes

[58] ctbto.org/press-centre/highlights/2011/fukushima-related-measurements-by-the-ctbto/fukushima-related-measurements-by-the-ctbto-page-1/

initially acting as a dividing line between the northern and southern air masses. As of 13 April 2011, radioactivity had spread to the southern hemisphere of the Asia-Pacific region and had been detected at stations located for example in Australia, Fiji, Malaysia and Papua New Guinea."[59]

Pretty much global coverage via clouds and air. For the record, travel by seawater takes longer...

---

[59] ctbto.org/press-centre/highlights/2011/fukushima-related-measurements-by-the-ctbto/fukushima-related-measurements-by-the-ctbto-page-1/

RADIOACTIVE SEAWATER &
MASSIVE ANIMAL DIE-OFFS

"The Fukushima nuclear complex went on to become the worst man-made engineering disaster in all of human history, outside of war."

— Steven Magee

Following the March 2011 Fukushima power plant meltdowns, TEPCO "estimated that the facility had released a staggering 7,000 trillion becquerels – a measure of emitted radiation – into nearby seawater. Meanwhile, Japan's Ministry of the Environment reported readings of 45.5 million becquerels per cubic meter of water, high enough to cause reproductive problems in fish."[60]

Researchers at California State University released a study in March 2012 in which they reported that as a result of the large amounts of radiation released from Fukushima into the atmosphere, a significant amount of radioactive iodine-131 was introduced into the kelp ecosystem in the Southern California coastal area.[61]

---

[60] sciencemag.org/news/2014/11/fukushima-radiation-nears-california-coast-judged-harmless

[61] Environ. Sci. Technol. 2012, 46, 7, 3731-3736

Chernobyl times 4

In May 2012, TEPCO released a report about radioactive discharges which seemed to show that "its Fukushima reactor has released more than quadruple the amount of radioactive cesium-137 leaked during the Chernobyl disaster. But the method used to measure the damage may undervalue the hazard even further" by only including measurements of cesium-131 and cesium-137 instead of all radioactive materials discharged... which would seem to show that Fukushima "amounts to 4 Chernobyls."[62]

Canada 2013

The National Academy of Sciences of the United States released a study at the end of 2014 that showed that radioactive seawater from Fukushima reached the continental shelf of Canada by June 2013.[63]

A marine chemist at Woods Hole Oceanographic Institute, Ken Buesseler, who was not involved in the study, noted that "Even when levels are small like this, it is important to collect systematic data so we can better predict how another event might move through the ocean."[64]

United States 2014

In November 2014, "Fukushima radiation had been identified in 10 offshore samples, including one 100

---

[62] rt.com/news/fukushima-chernobyl-cesium-137-contamination-145/

[63] Fukushima radioactivity transport to North America; John N. Smith, Robin M. Brown, William J. Williams, Marie Robert, Richard Nelson, S. Bradley Moran; Proceedings of the National Academy of Sciences Dec 2014, 201412814; DOI: 10.1073/pnas.1412814112

[64] phys.org/news/2014-12-tracking-fukushima-radioactivity-plume-pacific.html

miles off the coast of Eureka, California…"[65] Near the end of 2014, seawater containing radioactive contaminants reached areas near the West Coast of the United States including Alaska and the California coast.[66]

No human health risk

Leading health groups including "the World Health Organization and public health departments in California, Oregon, Washington, and Alaska all forecast that Fukushima radiation would not pose a human health risk in North America."[67] The operating term is "forecast" – you know, like those daily weather forecasts that always turn out so accurately…

Loads of data and "no reason" for concern

According to the citizen-science/crowd-funding effort dubbed OurRadioactiveOcean.org,

> "Perhaps the biggest news of 2015 is that we have begun seeing more sites, especially offshore where we have expanded our sampling, with contamination directly linked to Fukushima… almost any seawater sample from the Pacific will show traces of cesium-137, an isotope of cesium with a 30-year half-life, some of which is left over from nuclear weapons testing carried out in the 1950s to 1970s. The isotope cesium-134 is the 'fingerprint' of Fukushima, but it decays much

---

[65] dailyastorian.com/news/northwest/fukushima-radiation-has-reached-north-american-shores/article_d0bc8440-4b62-5819-b1c5-83fe134134ff.html

[66] whoi.edu/fileserver.do?id=197504&pt=2&p=205589

[67] sciencemag.org/news/2014/11/fukushima-radiation-nears-california-coast-judged-harmless

quicker (it has a 2-year half-life)... Our highest detection level to date came from a sample collected about 1,600 miles west of San Francisco... That (level) is 50 percent higher than we've seen before, but even these levels are still more than 500 times lower than safety limits established by the US government for drinking water and well below limits of concern for direct exposure while swimming, boating, or other recreational activities..."[68]

As far as any real danger outside the Fukushima region, they see nothing terribly alarming...

1,000,000 tons of radioactive water

By November 2018, the increasingly concerned International Atomic Energy Agency (IAEA) was urging TEPCO to address the roughly 1,000,000 tons of "treated" but still radioactive water TEPCO is storing at Fukushima.[69] While certain so-called nuclear experts felt the only real option to deal with the radioactive water was to – *wait for it* – release it into the Pacific... "fishermen and residents, however, strongly oppose the proposal..."[70] *Add in the rest of the world...*

While TEPCO claims they did conduct proper and careful treatments on the stored radioactive water, the radioactive water was still radioactive and was "not clean enough. It said the water contains cancer-causing

---

[68] ourradioactiveocean.org

[69] dailyastorian.com/news/world/iaea-urges-quick-plan-on-fukushima-radioactive-water-cleanup/article_9a6bc9ce-cf45-569e-8ec9-52f7f1a0dbfb.html

[70] dailyastorian.com/news/world/iaea-urges-quick-plan-on-fukushima-radioactive-water-cleanup/article_9a6bc9ce-cf45-569e-8ec9-52f7f1a0dbfb.html

cesium and other elements in excess of allowable limits for release into the environment."[71]

Could any of this affect animal health? Even just a little?

Massive animal die-offs a COMPLETE coincidence?
2017 saw massive animal die-offs on California beaches and coastline:

- "Hundreds of sick and dying seabirds and seals have been washing up on beaches in Ventura and Santa Barbara counties... Santa Barbara Wildlife Care Network estimated hundreds of pelicans and loons have died... blamed on domoic acid, which is a naturally occurring toxin in plankton that fish eat. Then other marine wildlife eats the fish."[72]

- "Hundreds Of Dead Seabirds, Sea Lions Wash Up In Southern California... Something disturbing has been washing up on Southern California beaches in recent weeks: dead and dying seabirds and marine mammals, numbering in the dozens."[73]

- "A flood of calls started over the weekend as beachgoers spotted sick or dying sea lions stranded on local beaches... Authorities say unusually high numbers of stranded or dead marine mammals and birds have shown up in

---

[71] dailyastorian.com/news/world/iaea-urges-quick-plan-on-fukushima-radioactive-water-cleanup/article_9a6bc9ce-cf45-569e-8ec9-52f7f1a0dbfb.html
[72] losangeles.cbslocal.com/2017/05/29/sick-dead-seabirds-pelicans-ventura-santa-barbara/
[73] huffingtonpost.com/entry/seabirds-sea-lions-california_us_592e8055e4b055a197ce440a

spots throughout the Southern California coast in recent weeks."[74]

- "Hundreds of dead puffins are mysteriously washing ashore in Alaska... Higher temperatures tend to result in fewer, smaller and less fatty zooplankton, the tiny organisms that many fish rely on for survival... That, in turn, leads to less prey for seabirds."[75]

- "'In the past three years, there have been massive die-offs of several different kinds of seabirds along the West Coast of the U.S. and in Alaska... The die-offs have spanned from San Francisco now up into the Bering Sea. And they have collectively killed perhaps a million birds,' indicating 'major shifts in the marine ecosystem' in the entire North Pacific...." concern "that the ecosystem shifts associated with ocean warming are profound, lasting and very negative at least for some species."[76]

Sorry - no funds in California to find out why

NBC reported on October 3, 2017, that "thousands of sharks and other sea life" including 500 bat rays, hundreds of striped bass, and 100 halibut died quite mysteriously in San Francisco Bay.

Did anyone really care to determine why? Not really. NBC asked and the "California Department of Fish and Wildlife says determining the cause is not a priority and,

---

[74] vcstar.com/story/news/special-reports/outdoors/2017/04/20/toxin-likely-blame-sea-lion-bird-deaths-ventura-county-california/100669606/
[75] huffingtonpost.com/entry/dead-puffins-st-paul-alaska-climate-change_us_582ea97ce4b099512f823237
[76] huffingtonpost.com/entry/dead-puffins-st-paul-alaska-climate-change_us_582ea97ce4b099512f823237

therefore, the state is not dedicating any funds towards researching the deaths..."[77]

Seriously?

Just betting that if cute Labrador puppies or safe-space comfort-pigs were keeling over by the thousands the response would have been very different...

But something fishy *is* going on world-wide as well
2017 was not only a bad month to be a fish near California, it was a world-wide mess – and the following is a sampling of strange fish and other animal die-offs that happened in *just* October 2017 alone...

- On beaches in Brazil, a report from South America detailed a record-breaking 103 whales that "stranded" themselves and died. A researcher noted that whales may be dying off as they encounter "an environment more and more altered by human activities, which can also cause strandings and deaths, fishing with nets, collisions with large vessels, mainly where the routes of ships that demand ports cross the concentration areas of humpbacks, and even the noise of certain activities, such as seismic prospecting, as well as pollution..."[78] In the same article, a veterinarian suggested that the culprit might be a decline in krill – "small crustaceans

---

[77] nbcbayarea.com/investigations/Thousands-of-Sharks-Other-Sea-Life-Mysteriously-Die-in-San-Francisco-Bay-State-Says-No-Funding-Available-to-Determine-Cause-449096583.html

[78] correio24horas.com.br/noticia/nid/por-que-tantas-baleias-encalharam-no-brasil-em-2017/

that serve as the main food of humpbacks in the Southern Hemisphere..."[79]

- In the municipality of Francisco Dumont, Brazil, hundreds of fish (plus cows, poultry, and wild birds) suddenly died after a short 5-minute-long hail and rain storm.[80]
- Thailand saw "tens of tons" of dead fish wash up on the Hua Hin beaches.[81]
- The Mersin district in southern Turkey saw hundreds of dead fish wash ashore baffling health officials.[82]
- Crayfish in large numbers were found dead in Ireland in River Barrow.[83]
- Thousands of dead fish washed up on the banks of the Río Negro in Uruguay.[84]
- Over in India, 5,000 Tilapia fish were found dead in a Mahbubsagar lake.[85]
- Thousands of marine animals including fish washed up on Maharashtra beach in India.[86]
- In Paraguay, up to 10,000 fish died in a river by Asuncion.[87]

---

[79] correio24horas.com.br/noticia/nid/por-que-tantas-baleias-encalharam-no-brasil-em-2017/

[80] g1.globo.com/mg/grande-minas/noticia/centenas-de-peixes-aves-e-gado-foram-encontrados-mortos-em-comunidades-de-francisco-dumont.ghtml

[81] bangkokpost.com/news/general/1344140/tonnes-of-dead-fish-wash-up-on-hua-hin-beach

[82] aksam.com.tr/yasam/silifkede-yuzlerce-balik-karaya-vurdu/haber-665705

[83] leinsterexpress.ie/news/local-news/273843/crayfish-plague-alert-as-large-numbers-of-dead-fish-reported-in-river-barrow.html

[84] lr21.com.uy/ecologia/1347975-peces-muertos-rio-negro-represa-palmar

[85] deccanchronicle.com/nation/current-affairs/171017/5000-fish-found-dead-in-mahbubsagar.html

[86] hindustantimes.com/mumbai-news/here-s-why-dead-fish-marine-animals-are-washing-up-maharashtra-shores/story-N9RxH40FpB9G4Dcycav5TK.html

[87] elpais.com/internacional/2017/10/17/america/1508245368_231773.html

- Across the ocean in Portugal, thousands of dead fish clogged the River Tagus.[88]
- 132 dead seals washed up on the shores of Lake Baikal in Russia.[89]
- Australia saw thousands of dead fish wash up in Sydney.[90]
- On an open-air fish farm in Scotland, 125,000 salmon died.[91]
- Some 80 tons of fish died in Viet Nam's Red River following a flood.[92]
- Tens of thousands of dead jelly-fish washed up on South Island in New Zealand.[93]
- Israel's Lakhish River filled up with thousands of dead fish.[94]
- Italy's Simeto river saw hundreds of dead fish wash up on its shores.[95]
- In Namibia, 100+ hippos dropped dead.[96]
- In Galicia, Spain, seagulls died by the hundreds.[97]

---

[88] rtp.pt/noticias/pais/milhares-de-peixes-mortos-no-tejo_v1033459

[89] interfax.ru/russia/585454

[90] dailytelegraph.com.au/newslocal/southern-courier/schools-of-dead-fish-have-washed-up-in-malabar-bay-polluting-the-popular-ocean-pool/news-story/6db50baf9306f652230f1583640ec0e3

[91] bbc.com/news/uk-scotland-highlands-islands-41689173

[92] vnexpress.net/tin-tuc/thoi-su/gan-80-tan-ca-long-chet-trang-tren-song-hong-sau-lu-3657090.html   vnexpress.net/tin-tuc/thoi-su/gan-80-tan-ca-long-chet-trang-tren-song-hong-sau-lu-3657090.html

[93] telegraph.co.uk/news/2017/10/14/thousands-jelly-creatures-wash-new-zealand-beaches/

[94] web.archive.org/web/20171013105821/https://www.jerusalemonline.com/news/in-israel/health-and-environment/lakhish-river-thousands-of-dead-fish-due-to-pollution-31652

[95] catania.meridionews.it/articolo/59511/oasi-simeto-centinaia-di-pesci-morti-in-riva-al-fiume-legambiente-e-inquietante-si-attendono-analisi/

[96] bbc.com/news/world-africa-41558385

[97] lavozdegalicia.es/noticia/sociedad/2017/10/06/biologos-apuntan-botulismo-causa-muerte-gaviotas-litoral/0003_201710G6P28991.htm

- In Bali, after a long rain shower, thousands of sparrows suddenly dropped dead and fell from the sky onto the streets of Bongaja.[98]
- 300 tons of fish suddenly died in open-air fish farms in Cianjur, Indonesia.[99]

We could go on and on, but you get the picture. Again, that was just a sample of die-offs in October 2017. At a minimum it's super weird...

While many scientists say they are baffled and often can't explain the causes of the massive die-offs, some explanations and "what to blame" range from toxins and pesticides, warmer temperatures, and climate change, to infections, diseases, and depleted oxygen levels, to natural phenomenon and freak accidents, from a shortage of food supplies and natural cycles, to toxic gas, parasites, and disease.

The question no one seems to ask

No conspiracy theories here, but did you notice what's missing? Some may think those new "5G" cellular networks beaming out millimeter-sized microwaves, or, maybe, those chemtrails sprayed across the skies are involved. Perhaps.

But we're specifically asking about *radiation*. How about some real scientific investigation into whether radioactive particles released into the sea or air from the Fukushima disaster might have contributed to, and may still be contributing to mass die-offs?

---

[98] tribunnews.com/regional/2017/09/26/ribuan-burung-pipit-mati-mendadak-di-bali-ini-kaitannya-dengan-status-awas-gunung-agung

[99] liputan6.com/news/read/3111040/ratusan-ton-ikan-mati-mendadak-di-cianjur

Record-setting discharge a coincidence?
Back in October 2011, the Institute for Radiological Protection and Nuclear Safety released a report revealing that the nuclear disaster at Fukushima had released the largest discharge of radioactive material into the ocean in recorded history.[100]

Read that again. "The Largest Discharge of Radioactive Material into the Ocean in Recorded History."

Food chain snowball effect
The report also explained that the highest concentration of radioactivity would start in the smaller ocean species and work its way up the food chain so that "it will be the predators at the top of the food chain that should show the higher levels" of radiation contamination cautioning that "even though cesium contamination in seawater has greatly decreased near the Fukushima Daiichi plant, it is justified to maintain a surveillance of the marine species fished in the coastal waters off the northeast coast of Japan..."[101]

More no-comments
Bloomberg Business also added that the Institute for Radiological Protection and Nuclear Safety report was the "second report released in a week calling into question estimates from Japan's government and the operator of the plant that was damaged in the March earthquake and tsunami. The Fukushima station may have emitted more than double the company's estimate

---

[100] irsn.fr/FR/Actualites_presse/Actualites/Documents/IRSN-NI-Impact_accident_Fukushima_sur_milieu_marin_26102011.pdf
[101] irsn.fr/FR/Actualites_presse/Actualites/Documents/IRSN-NI-Impact_accident_Fukushima_sur_milieu_marin_26102011.pdf

of atmospheric release at the height of the worst civil atomic crisis since Chernobyl in 1986...” Asked to comment, the response was that “TEPCO is aware of the estimate from the institute through media reports and has no comment...”[102]

Naturally...

So animals, especially sea animals, are dying off in droves yet the largest release of radioactive gunk in oceanographic history has NOTHING to do with it??

Seriously??

Well at least our politicians will keep us safe...

---

[102] web.archive.org/web/20160205060653/http://www.bloomberg.com/news/articles/2011-10-31/fukushima-plant-released-record-amount-of-radiation-into-ocean

RADIOACTIVE HILLARY, JAPANESE FOOD SUPPLIES, AND U.S. WATER, RAIN, & MILK

"Pls print."

— Hillary Rodham Clinton
Unclassified released email archive
US Department of State[103]

On Tuesday March 22, 2011, then-Secretary-of-State Hillary Rodham Clinton sent an email to a staffer to print out a report on Fukushima. The email, "Subject: Fw: A Must Read, on Japan from The Economist," seemed to be a text version of an article that noted, "The magnitude-9 earthquake—the largest ever in the country's history, equivalent in power to 30,000 Hiroshimas—was followed by a wave which wiped out whole towns... the scale of the horror is still sinking in. The surge of icy water shoved the debris of destroyed towns miles inland, killing most of those too old or too slow to scramble to higher ground..."

Is this proof that Hillary knew only too well about the Fukushima disaster? Was it on her radar screen? How about any possibility of radioactive contamination of

---

[103] foia.state.gov/Learn/New.aspx

products headed for the US? For instance, did Hillary know anything about potentially contaminated food?

Downplaying the disaster

In a shocking and mostly ignored revelation, someone named Arnie Gundersen revealed in a radio interview in 2011 on Solar IMG[104] that, according to his high-level source in the State Department, "the United States Government has come up with a decision, and I don't know whether it's influenced by a fear of panic or a commercial interests or whatever, but I do know that the United States Government at the highest levels of the State Department, as well as other departments, FDA, and on and on, have made a decision to downplay Fukushima."[105]

By the way, the original interview link and interview have mysteriously disappeared but luckily was available on a large back-up site... Hmmm....

Hold on... Secret plans to downplay a nuclear accident and its aftereffects? *Come on.* So who is Gundersen? Some sort of conspiracy flake, right?

Actually, no. *Hell* no!

With over 45-years of experience in nuclear power engineering, Gundersen is currently a "nuclear engineer and expert witness... (and) the chief engineer for Fairewinds Associates, Inc., paralegal services and

---

[104] web.archive.org/web/20120127150635/http://www.solarimg.org/shows/SolarIMG_podcast_Arnie_Gundersen_130811.mp3

[105] web.archive.org/web/20120127150635/http://www.solarimg.org/shows/SolarIMG_podcast_Arnie_Gundersen_130811.mp3

expert testimony firm as well as a member of Fairewinds Energy Education's Board of Directors...[106] He's worked on projects at over 70 US nuclear power plants and even holds a patent for a nuclear safety device. Still not convinced? Gundersen also held a license to "operate a nuclear reactor"[107] issued by the U.S. Atomic Energy Commission. How many of *your* friends can say that?

Ok, ok, geez, so he's super *credible... So what?*

Actually a BIG what...

Sign on the dotted line
According to Gundersen, not only did the US Government decide to intentionally gloss over the Fukushima incident, but then-Secretary-of-State Hillary Clinton and her Japanese counterpart actually "signed a pact" in which Clinton "agreed that there are no problems with Japanese food supplies and we would continue to buy them... so we are *not* sampling this material as it comes into the country because our Government, the US, has made a decision, a strategic decision, to downplay it..."[108]

So on behalf of all of us trusting US taxpayers, Hillary apparently agreed that, after a monumental nuclear disaster spewing radioactive residue all over the place, the United States would *continue to buy food* from Japan

---

[106] fairewinds.org/about-us/

[107] fairewinds.org/meet-the-crew/

[108] web.archive.org/web/20120127150635/http://www.solarimg.org/shows/SolarIMG_podcast_Arnie_Gundersen_130811.mp3

even though the food *wouldn't be tested* for radioactivity…

Seriously. Read that again.

Where was the mainstream media?

Taiwan ain't buyin' it…
In the meanwhile, Taiwan didn't really care much about offending anyone and, instead, was taking no chances with the health of its people. So, Taiwan officially banned food imports from the Fukushima regions affected by the nuclear disaster.

Even though the Japanese claimed in late 2018 that Taiwan had checked thousands of food samples for radiation and had found none that exceeded legal regulations, Taiwan voted in late November 2018 to *continue its ban*… which really pissed off Japan's Foreign Minister who threatened to complain to the World Trade Organization about Taiwan…[109]

US drinking water and more
In April 2011 the US EPA (Environmental Protection Agency) issued data that they had detected Fukushima radiation in the *drinking water* of 13 US cities; in *rainwater* samples from Utah, Massachusetts, Alabama, and Idaho; in the *air* in Alabama, Alaska, Idaho, and Nevada; and in milk from cows in Arizona, California, and Vermont. The radioactivity of one milk sample was

---

[109] japantimes.co.jp/news/2018/12/02/national/politics-diplomacy/japan-may-take-taiwans-fukushima-food-import-ban-wto/

over and one was *just below* the maximum permitted contamination level set by the EPA.[110]

The Wall Street Journal reported that the "EPA said it found minuscule traces of a radioactive isotope in California that appeared to come from the Fukushima plant. The EPA has since detected similarly low levels of radiation in other locations" and "will continue to monitor radiation drifting to the U.S. from a damaged nuclear plant in Japan..."[111]

Oh. Ok. At least it's only food, water, and air. Because if it included cars, man, that would really suck...

---

[110] forbes.com/sites/jeffmcmahon/2011/04/09/radiation-detected-in-drinking-water-in-13-more-us-cities-cesium-137-in-vermont-milk/

[111] blogs.wsj.com/washwire/2011/04/08/epa-keeps-tracking-japan-radiation/

RADIOACTIVE CONTAINERS & CARS

"I've always been asked, 'What is my favorite car?' and I've always said 'The next one.'"

— Carroll Shelby

In May 2011 Longshore Shipping & News noted that radiation was found by Dutch authorities in Rotterdam on 19 containers shipped from Japan. 5 containers had to be "quarantined because the level of contamination was above the permissible threshold, the Dutch Food and Consumer Product Safety Authority said…"[112]

Not good.

Did you hear the main stream media raising any alarms or focusing on the possible ramifications?

Used cars
In an October 26, 2011 article titled "Radioactive second-hand cars dog Japan," the Asia Editor of The Times newspaper of London, Richard Lloyd Parry, wrote about a strange situation created in Japan by the Fukushima meltdown.

---

[112] longshoreshippingnews.com/2011/05/japanese-containers-test-positive-for-radiation-on-arrival-in-rotterdam/

It appears that many vehicles in the area absorbed nuclear radiation from Fukushima. Parry explained that "in the aftermath of the nuclear disaster, used-car dealerships have found themselves stuck with vehicles that have absorbed high levels of radiation from the meltdown of the reactors at the Fukushima nuclear plant." What to do?

Shockingly, instead of disposing of the toxic cars, dealers apparently re-registered them to hide ties to Fukushima, and tried to sell them to unsuspecting consumers or to export them.

If you can't get rid of the radiation, make a plan
The expose revealed that a journalist "tracked down the dealer who first bought the notoriously radioactive van for 1.43 million yen ($A18,100) at a wholesale auction, only to discover that it emitted radiation at a level of 110 microsieverts an hour... (the car dealer) told the newspaper: 'I decontaminated repeatedly after the test, and retested the filter of the air conditioner, the wipers and tires, replacing them thoroughly, but the radiation level dropped only to 30 microsieverts per hour. I decided to sell the vehicle in Japan because I couldn't afford to lose the money." [113] He eventually sold the van hundreds of miles away from Fukushima. In the meanwhile, regulations appear to have been toughened up with a new export limit of 0.3 microsieverts...

Africa on alert
In August 2012, Uganda's Daily Monitor revealed that "a large number of second hand radioactive vehicles that

---

[113] web.archive.org/web/20120505133636/https://www.theaustralian.com.au/news/world/radioactive-second-hand-cars-dog-japan/story-e6frg6so-1226177000267

originated from Japan's exclusion zone that surrounds the Fukushima prefecture's power plant have made their way into the used car market in the country."[114]
Sadly, officials from Uganda had previously known about the dangers of radiation having visited Japan where "…it was established, through random scientific tests as well as motor vehicle inspection records, that many used motor vehicles destined for export markets from Japan, are contaminated with significantly high levels of ionizing radiation, way above recommended levels."[115]

The Ugandan officials also were made aware during their visit that "gamma radiation contamination cannot be cleaned off the affected surface and it has high penetrative strength, for instance, the ability to penetrate through any material, say a layer of concrete three metres thick."[116]

Other African countries, such as Tanzania and Kenya, had already preemptively blocked the importation of used-cars from Japan.

Russia
On October 24, 2011, it was reported that customs officials in eastern Russia discovered about 50 used-

---

[114] monitor.co.ug/News/National/Radioactive-Japanese-cars-on-the-market/688334-1487016-suvsj8/index.html
[115] monitor.co.ug/News/National/Radioactive-Japanese-cars-on-the-market/688334-1487016-suvsj8/index.html
[116] monitor.co.ug/News/National/Radioactive-Japanese-cars-on-the-market/688334-1487016-suvsj8/index.html

cars shipped from Japan "with radiation levels up to six times above normal."[117]

Chile just hoses it off

The Seattle Times warned in May of 2011 that "Customs agents in Chile have detected low levels of radioactivity in cars shipped from" Japan. While port workers, concerned with their health, protested, "the Chilean nuclear commission confirmed that the radioactivity is too low to cause damage to humans... (and that) the cars will be hosed down on board and any radioactivity will be contained inside the ship." *Great plan...*

Down under

June 2011 saw Australia begin testing cars shipped in from Japan for radiation.[118] At that time, a physician nominated for the Nobel Peace Prize commented that the testing was "scientifically negligent" and that "the best way to properly detect radiation in vehicles was to remove and test engine and passenger compartment air filters."[119] In one case involving 103 cars, apparently inspectors had only tested one car's engine filter, scanning another 102 cars in a far less thorough manner. Lax is lax...

Gee, just wondering, wouldn't health professionals worldwide be up in arms about even a few of these radioactive revelations?

---

[117] enformable.com/2011/10/radiation-effects-japanese-automobile-effects-international-authorities-checking-imports-dealers-selling-radioactive-used-cars-in-japan/

[118] caradvice.com.au/123945/australian-vehicles-imported-from-japan-to-be-radiation-tested/

[119] longshoreshippingnews.com/2011/06/doctor-says-australias-radiation-test-on-cars-scientifically-negligent/

RADIOACTIVE HEALTH

"Ignore the glowing dust, folks. Stay in line and don't straggle. Keep it moving. Nothing to see here...."

— Main Stream Media script

Hey, if this Fukushima thing is really so bad, wouldn't medical doctors be raising the alarm?

How about radio talk show hosts?

And Nobel-Prize-worthy super smart thinkers?

Well actually, yes...

Meet radio show host and pediatrician, Dr. Helen Caldicott, M.D., who is dedicated to spreading what she understands as the truth about nuclear power. Oh, and yes, she's also a Nobel Peace Prize nominee....

In May 2015, Dr. Caldicott was a featured speaker at The Real Truth About Health Conference. She cautioned people that the dangers from Fukushima are real and only just starting...

Lessons from Chernobyl
First, Dr. Caldicott reported on some rather terrifying statistics from the Chernobyl nuclear disaster that happened in 1986 in the northern Ukraine area of the

old Soviet Union. She explained that radiation from the Chernobyl accident contaminated many specific areas in Europe beyond the Ukraine. Specifically, Dr. Caldicott mentioned Finland, Sweden, Norway, Germany, Belarus, and even parts of England. She reported that in the UK, 300 sheep farms were forced to close due to lambs contaminated with high levels of cesium from Chernobyl.

Dr. Caldicott went on to mention that Turkey apparently got a "huge fallout" and admonished attendees to not buy anything from Turkey since you wouldn't know what may be radioactive or not... In fact, Dr. Caldicott warned not to buy any food from Europe since you wouldn't know if it might have "cesium in it, or strontium in it, or plutonium in it."[120]

Here and now
Moving on to Fukushima, after vividly explaining how the accident happened and warning that the site would stay radioactive for hundreds of years, Dr. Caldicott focused on the aftermath as it relates to health and life.

It seems the core of the current and future troubles is that seawater continues to wash over the nuclear waste and is becoming more and more radioactive *daily* with no end in sight.

The contaminated seawater then passes the radiation along to ocean plants and animals. As the fish eat the contaminated plants and animals, they become contaminated, and as bigger fish eat the smaller fish, the

---

[120] youtube.com/watch?v=-ZcbpMekls4

radiation keeps being passed along... According to Dr. Caldicott, tuna with Fukushima radiation have already shown up in California.

Mincing no words
"Don't go to Japan," and don't eat any food from Japan says Dr. Caldicott who is concerned that even if you were to visit the south of Japan, further away from Fukushima, you still wouldn't know where the food is sourced from. She also predicts children in the region will be coming down with all sorts of medical issues related to Fukushima radiation.

Is this all just over-cautious paranoia?

Maybe, maybe not. When you take into account that "radiation reached such elevated levels that the robots tasked with cleaning the reactor could not survive..."[121] you perk up and listen...

Seriously, when *robots* can't handle the radiation levels, well, it can't be good... and it's not.

---

[121] ibtimes.com/fukushima-japan-ban-fish-exports-over-after-nuclear-radiation-disaster-countries-2508805

RADIOACTIVE ROBOTS

"Fukushima News: 'Unimaginable' Nuclear Reactor Radiation So Destructive, Not Even Robots Can Survive."

—International Business Times 2/10/17

In December 2016, Tokyo Electric Power Company (TEPCO) increased its estimated cost to complete the cleanup operation to a staggering $188 billion[122]... double the previous estimate.

And that was before robot-killing radiation was discovered...

When robots die

In March 2017, according to the president in charge of the Fukushima Daiichi Decommissioning project, they needed to create a more radiation-tolerant robot since "the exploratory robot, specially designed to navigate the underwater sections of the reactor, died last month after being exposed to 'unimaginable' levels of radiation nearly nine times more potent than the previous highest dose recorded."[123]

---

[122] ibtimes.com/fukushima-news-unimaginable-nuclear-reactor-radiation-so-destructive-not-even-robots-2489802

[123] ibtimes.com/fukushima-news-deadly-nuclear-radiation-levels-baffle-scientists-trying-build-robot-2502250

Highest radiation levels ever

So instead of dissipating, these latest radiation levels had increased about 900% over the highest levels ever recorded since the meltdown...

The Japan Times had noted in February 2017 that these new radiation levels "could kill a person quickly and indicates the fuel likely burned through the pressure vessel during the meltdown and is somewhere nearby..."[124]

According to a report in the International Business Times, "The previous high was measured one year after the disaster at 73 Sieverts per hour. Recent measurements showed levels of 650 Sieverts per hour. A dose of 10 Sieverts would likely cause death within weeks."[125]

The Asahi Shimbun opined that decommissioning operations could face more delays due to "radiation levels that can kill a person in a minute and holes created by melted nuclear fuel..." and reported that "TEPCO said it will need 30 to 40 years to complete the decommissioning process. The utility plans to start work to remove the melted nuclear fuel at the No. 2 and two other stricken reactors in 2021 after deciding on a removal method in fiscal 2018..."[126]

Not good news.

---

[124] japantimes.co.jp/news/2017/02/10/national/high-radiation-readings-at-fukushima-no-2-reactor/

[125] ibtimes.com/fukushima-overrun-wild-boars-amid-radiation-nuclear-reactor-meltdown-2505287

[126] web.archive.org/web/20170630041923/http://www.asahi.com/ajw/articles/AJ20170 2030064.html

Given that Tokyo won the bid to host the 2020 Olympics, and that they plan to play some qualifying rounds for baseball in the Fukushima region (*yes, your read that right*), it isn't surprising that when any new evidence of badness emanates from Fukushima, politicians and officials jump on the offensive.

The facts prove true regardless of questions

So when these new record levels of radiation were reported, sure enough, officials started aggressively questioning the findings. But facts are facts and in the end, a government source told the Japan Times that "I had hoped that the previous results were wrong, but it is certain that there is an area with high radiation levels inside the reactor."[127]

Sending in new robots

In November 2017 TEPCO announced it had been able to locate the melted fuel with newly designed robots. The significance of locating the fuel was noted by the New York Times which reported that, "Six and a half years after the accident spewed radiation over northern Japan, and at one point seemed to endanger Tokyo, the officials hope to persuade a skeptical world that the plant has moved out of post-disaster crisis mode and into something much less threatening: cleanup."[128]

Please just tell me that the crews cleaning up radioactive materials are all carefully trained professionals. Like they're not homeless or migrants or refugees... Right?

---

[127] japantimes.co.jp/news/2017/02/10/national/high-radiation-readings-at-fukushima-no-2-reactor/

[128] nytimes.com/2017/11/19/science/japan-fukushima-nuclear-meltdown-fuel.html

RADIOACTIVE CONTRACTS

"In my lifetime, as a younger man, you were assumed to be an honest person. Your word was your bond, and a handshake was as good as a contract in business.

— Mark Skousen

In March 2013 it was discovered that the official cleanup efforts after the Fukushima Daiichi disaster might be failing for a very simple reason – "counterfeit contracts." *Sora News 24* reported in 2013 that "more than half of the laborers employed at the nuclear site are suspected of being involved in counterfeit contract work."[129]

Cleaning up radioactive materials is serious business requiring tight controls, specially trained employees, and meticulous monitoring.

So what are counterfeit contracts?

Subcontractors' subcontractors' subcontractors
Very simply, a company gets an initial contract to work on the cleanup efforts. Then they hire subcontractors. Then those subcontractors hire other subcontractors

---

[129] soranews24.com/2013/03/14/more-than-half-of-cleanup-staff-at-fukushima-nuclear-plant-on-counterfeit-contracts/

and according to *Sora News 24* this is "giving rise to a multiple subcontract working system where it is difficult to know who is really in charge. While the original subcontractor might well be operating legally, with multiple subcontracts overlapping in this way, the practice of passing designated work down from subcontractor to subcontractor ultimately creates a breeding ground for unscrupulous activity."[130]In response to this revelation, the Japanese government stated their intent to get a handle on things…

But as *Sora News 24* noted, "What compounds problems further is that the radiation exposure levels of many workers far exceed those being officially recorded."[131]

Tens of thousands of people have worked to clean up the Fukushima nuclear mess…

The Radiation Worker Central Registration Centre of Japan "showed that as many as 76,951 decontamination workers were hired in the five-year period up to 2016."[132]

United Nations sounds humanitarian alarms
On August 16, 2018, the United Nations issued alarming statements urging Japan to "urgently protect tens of thousands of workers hired to help decontaminate the

---

[130] soranews24.com/2013/03/14/more-than-half-of-cleanup-staff-at-fukushima-nuclear-plant-on-counterfeit-contracts/
[131] soranews24.com/2013/03/14/more-than-half-of-cleanup-staff-at-fukushima-nuclear-plant-on-counterfeit-contracts/
[132] news.un.org/en/story/2018/08/1017232

Fukushima nuclear plant, who are reportedly being exploited and exposed to toxic nuclear radiation."[133]

Motley crew including migrants and the homeless
The UN also expressed concern about possible "'exploitation' of the homeless and migrant workers during the Fukushima clean-up works."[134]

According to the UN, "workers hired to decontaminate Fukushima reportedly include migrant workers, asylum seekers and people who are homeless" and that the UN was "deeply concerned about possible exploitation by deception regarding the risks of exposure to radiation, possible coercion into accepting hazardous working conditions because of economic hardships, and the adequacy of training and protective measures."[135]

In 2018, many people were still working on cleanup efforts, with "about 5,000 people on average… (continuing) to work at the Fukushima plant per day, according to the Japanese NHK broadcaster."[136]

Russian collusion – at a snail's pace
Shortly after the Fukushima meltdown, in 2011, Russia reached out and offered to help Japan. Experience honed in their Chernobyl nuclear disaster could prove invaluable. Japan apparently didn't take up the offer. Why? Do they remain sore about a *still-active* dispute over territory with Russia dating back to WWII that has kept an official peace treaty at bay? *Who knows…*

---

[133] news.un.org/en/story/2018/08/1017232
[134] rt.com/news/437711-fukushima-radiation-exposure-death/
[135] news.un.org/en/story/2018/08/1017232
[136] rt.com/news/437711-fukushima-radiation-exposure-death/

Contaminating ground water and the ocean
Watching as TEPCO pumped tremendous amounts of water through the Fukushima facility to cool it, with the contaminated water "leaking into ground water and the ocean," in 2013 Russia again repeated its offer to help, stating that "the approach to cooling and decommissioning the station will need to change and include technologies developed outside of Japan if the cleanup is to succeed..."[137] A Russian nuclear utility director also stressed that we're all in this together as nuclear accidents are not national incidents but "they are all international" in scope. He added that "It was clear for a long time that TEPCO was not adequately coping with the situation..."[138] *Hurry up and wait.*

In 2017, Japanese Prime Minister Abe met in Moscow with Russian President Putin. They discussed working together to clean up Fukushima. President Putin noted that "Russia is ready to assist Japan in the Fukushima-1 nuclear power plant cleanup and offers the latest technologies for cleaning contaminated soil and reprocessing radioactive waste."[139] *Still waiting...*

Finally, in mid-January 2019, almost 8 years after the first offer to help from Russia, a Russian nuclear firm was chosen to assist Japan with the cleanup efforts going forward.[140] *You would think that with so much at stake, things might have moved a bit faster...*

---

[137] bloomberg.com/news/articles/2013-08-25/russia-offers-to-help-clean-up-fukushima-as-tepco-calls-for-help

[138] nuclear-news.net/2013/08/25/russia-offers-to-help-clean-up-fukushima-as-tepco-calls-for-help-but-russia-blames-others/

[139] sputniknews.com/world/201704271053078015-russia-japan-putin-fukushima/

[140] https://www.rt.com/business/448765-rosatom-bids-fukushima-npp/

RADIOACTIVE CENSORSHIP?

"In the central areas of the nearby villages and towns there is not a soul around. They are real cities of death."

— Yoshio Hachiro
Minister of Economy, Trade and Industry
(In his position only about a week, Hachiro predictably lost his job shortly after making this observation in September 2011...)[141]

When catastrophic stuff happens in Japan and you can't fix it fast enough, do you:
a) Warn everyone while you seek solutions
b) Ask international experts to assist you
c) Strive for transparency as you provide full and complete data
d) Welcome open and honest dialogue

or...

e) Do some of the above, while labeling serious questioners and investigators as dangerous irresponsible rumor-mongers that pose a danger to national and economic security, bar all internet and foreign media from official press conferences, and tell media outlets and internet platforms to censor and/or control any information on Fukushima that may make citizens "uneasy" or "fearful"...

---

[141] japantimes.co.jp/community/2011/12/27/general/2011-a-year-of-disaster-in-quotes

Of course, you guessed (e)...

Weeding out dissenters
Watching a potential economic and social tsunami whipping up fast, amidst ever increasing questions about the actual state of affairs in and around Fukushima, the Japanese Ministry of Internal Affairs and Communications issued a press release on April 6, 2011, which read in part:

> "The Ministry of Public Management, Home Affairs, Posts and Telecommunications today announced to telecommunications-carrier-related organizations that telecommunications carriers, etc. belonging to each group, to appropriately respond to the East Japan great earthquake disaster relief *fanciful chatter* considering freedom of expression and to take necessary measures..."[142]

Does that mean information critical of the handling of Fukushima efforts is somehow fake and should be disappeared?

> "In the same countermeasures, after the Great East Japan Earthquake, in consideration of the situation that dissident lullabies that rapture the citizens' uneasiness, such as uncertain information on earthquakes etc, are disseminated by writing to the electronic bulletin board etc., Ministries and agencies should cooperate and ask site administrators etc. to take appropriate measures including voluntary deletion of information

---

[142] soumu.go.jp/menu_news/s-news/01kiban08_01000023.html

contrary to public order and morality and strive to provide accurate information to users..."[143]

Does that sound as though the Ministry is, first, painting any narratives that are counter to "All is well" as dangerous nonsense, and second, making it clear to webmasters to delete that info "voluntarily"?

> "Based on the above countermeasures, the Ministry of Internal Affairs and Communications provides the Telecommunications Service Association, The Telecom Service Association, the Japan Internet Provider Association, and the Japan Cable Television Federation on the Internet on rumors on Great East Japan Earthquake, Telecommunications operators belonging to each group requested to make known and necessary measures to respond appropriately while considering freedom of expression."[144]

And doesn't that sound as if the Ministry is blanketly labeling any information, not to their liking, as just "internet rumors" that must be "responded to appropriately"?

BTW, anyone else notice that the Ministry was careful to include "considering freedom of expression" in its thinly veiled censorship decree? As if they were truly truth seekers simply attempting to stamp out lies and misinformation... *Charming, right?*

---

[143] soumu.go.jp/menu_news/s-news/01kiban08_01000023.html

[144] soumu.go.jp/menu_news/s-news/01kiban08_01000023.html

Diametrically opposed views

The Asia-Pacific Journal reported on April 18, 2011 that "many local officials and residents in Fukushima insist that the situation is safe and that the media, in fanning unwarranted fears, are damaging the economy of the region. By contrast, many freelance journalists in Tokyo report that the central government is downplaying the fact that radiation leakage has been massive and that the threat to public health has been woefully underestimated."[145]

Indeed, although the Japanese government itself had reported on April 12, 2011, that "the Fukushima radiation severity level has been raised from a level 5 event (as with Three Mile Island) to a level 7 event (as with Chernobyl), the government also extended the radiation exclusion zone from 20 kilometers to at least five communities in the 30-50 kilometer range..."[146]

So the Japanese government admits that the nuclear disaster level is really 40% worse than they previously reported, and that the very real and dangerous radiation exclusion zone would now be extended to 150% to 250% further out than previously set... adding another 5 new communities to the danger zone... and the reaction is what? Caution? Abandonment?

How's about some head-in-the-sand-ism...

Fearmongering blamed for economic losses

Unbelievably, many locals apparently felt all was fine... many returned to their homes in the high radiation

---

[145] apjjf.org/-Makiko-Segawa/3516/article.pdf

[146] apjjf.org/-Makiko-Segawa/3516/article.pdf

exclusion zones. According to The Asia-Pacific Journal, schools held regular entrance ceremonies, dairy farmers got back to business but lamented the drop in activity, politicians grieved over economic downturns, and locals blamed the media and fearmongering for ruining the local economy as businesses faltered and unemployment went up.

The PR director for one of the affected cities stated that "Since harmful rumors are so powerful, not only are farming and fishing industries affected, even some industries have been damaged as a result of claims that even machines are contaminated!"[147]

Sing "all is well" or don't sing at all

The common theme seems to be that "all is well" and anyone who doesn't agree is part of the problem. It's not the nuclear radiation that is at fault. It isn't the radioactive fallout on the ground, or radioactive contamination of the plants and animals, or the radioactive waste all over the place. NO! It's the people *noticing it* that are the real problem...

The locals have been pointed in the *All-Is-Well* direction by more than just the government. For instance, on April 6, 2011 at a school entrance ceremony in Iwaki City, *well within the official radiation zone*, and LESS THAN a month after one of the world's worst nuclear accidents, a school doctor boldly assured students and parents that *All-Is-Well* and that "radiation leakages from the Fukushima Daiichi plant were decreasing and would soon fade away..." (soon FADE away???) and that

---

[147] apjjf.org/-Makiko-Segawa/3516/article.pdf

"The radiation problem is already finished... You can go to school and go outside without any problem. You should not fear malicious gossip."[148] Really?

Got it? Nuclear radiation simply fades away and that anyone that warns of the dangers of radiation is simply spreading "malicious gossip."

Was the US any better?

Evasion and subterfuge?
In March 2014, NBC News stated that after reviewing thousands of emails they obtained through the Freedom of Information Act, reporters concluded that "staff at the U.S. Nuclear Regulatory Commission (NRC) made a concerted effort to play down the risk of earthquakes and tsunamis to America's aging nuclear plants." NBC News bluntly highlighted "numerous examples in the emails of apparent misdirection or concealment..."[149]

Stick to the story
NBC reported that "NRC Public Affairs Director Eliot Brenner thanked his staff for sticking to the talking points that the team had been distributing to senior officials and the public... 'While we know more than these say,' Brenner wrote,' we're sticking to this story for now.'"[150]

Unbelievable...

---

[148] apjjf.org/-Makiko-Segawa/3516/article.pdf

[149] nbcnews.com/storyline/fukushima-anniversary/u-s-nuclear-agency-hid-concerns-hailed-safety-record-fukushima-n48561

[150] nbcnews.com/storyline/fukushima-anniversary/u-s-nuclear-agency-hid-concerns-hailed-safety-record-fukushima-n48561

PR nightmare

Why the efforts to tone down events? NBC figured out the "NRC staff recognized immediately the public-relations nightmare that Fukushima presented for nuclear power in the United States. More than 30 of America's 100 nuclear power reactors have the same brand of General Electric reactors or containment system used in Fukushima..."

Obama administration lays low

Surprisingly, NBC found that the "emails indicate that the Obama administration and the NRC were keen to keep up the appearance that they were merely observing the Japanese nuclear crisis and had no responsibility for helping resolve it."[151] Concurrently, Japanese engineers were physically at the NRC but staff were told "While one reporter knows or has guessed that there are Japanese here in our Ops center in communication with their home authorities, we will NOT make the[m] available and we will NOT volunteer their presence."

Discredit the reporters

In a twist worthy of the old Soviet Politburo, according to NBC, "the NRC's Public Affairs staff attempted to discredit news reports that raised questions about nuclear plants, even when they were based on NRC data..."[152]

Wow.

---

[151] nbcnews.com/storyline/fukushima-anniversary/u-s-nuclear-agency-hid-concerns-hailed-safety-record-fukushima-n48561

[152] nbcnews.com/storyline/fukushima-anniversary/u-s-nuclear-agency-hid-concerns-hailed-safety-record-fukushima-n48561

If you don't check for radiation, you won't find it.
In a very disturbing complication, "NOAA suspended testing in the Pacific for Fukushima radiation last summer after concluding that there wasn't any radiation to be detected..."[153]

> "As far as questions about radiation, we are working with radiation experts within the Environmental Protection Agency and the Department of Energy.... NOAA is not currently doing further research on seafood... NOAA is doing a study related to radiation that is focused on radiation plume modeling."
>
> NOAA media liaison Keeley Belva[154]

As EnviroReporter Michael Collins noted, "In other words, no federal agency, department or administration is doing anything to sample and analyze water from the Pacific. Fish aren't being tested for contamination, either."[155]

The faithless gather their own data
In March 2018 PhysOrg reported that many people in Japan had lost faith in official government stories about Fukushima. Some had started to simply take their own readings. "Citizen scientists" across Japan now help gather real-time data with Geiger counters. One such citizen, who had been measuring radiation levels since 2007, said "The (Japanese) government didn't tell us the truth, they didn't tell us the true measures... the readings were so high... 50 times higher than natural

---

[153] seecalifornia.com/news/fukushima-disaster-and-its-global-reach/
[154] seecalifornia.com/news/fukushima-disaster-and-its-global-reach/
[155] seecalifornia.com/news/fukushima-disaster-and-its-global-reach/

radiation... I was amazed... the news was telling us there was nothing, the administration was telling us there was nothing to worry about..."[156]

Another citizen scientist explained that he had initially stayed in his town since it was safely outside the official evacuation zone established by the Japanese government. Other evacuees also went to that town. Yet after he started taking radiation readings he discovered "there was a high level of risk here as well." Although "he sent his children away ...(he) stayed behind to look after his mother, a decision he believes may have contributed to his 2015 diagnosis with thyroid cancer."[157]

All the measured radioactivity data is fed to an NGO named Safecast which relies on this network of citizen scientists who volunteer to help.

One of the founders of Safecast stated that, "Our volunteers decide to measure where their schools are, where their workplaces are, where their houses are," and hopes Safecast will help make the government of Japan realize that "transparency and being open are very important to create trust."

One citizen scientist fears for the safety of people, especially students, who may not know areas are dangerous and said "If there are no people like me who continue to monitor the levels, it will be forgotten."

Forgotten? More like swept under the carpet...

---

[156] phys.org/news/2018-03-citizen-scientists-track-years-fukushima.html

[157] phys.org/news/2018-03-citizen-scientists-track-years-fukushima.html

RADIOACTIVE DUST & SOIL

"Fukushima fallout appeared to affect all areas of the U.S., and was especially large in some, mostly in the western part of the nation."

Joseph J. Mangano & Janette D. Sherman

Scientist, civil engineer, and researcher Marco Kaltofen with the Worcester Polytechnic Institute in Massachusetts revealed in late October 2011 that he had determined that radioactive dust from the Fukushima disaster was the likely source of "human exposure to radiation."[158] He presented his findings at the American Public Health Association noting that people can be exposed to radioactive particles by inhaling them directly from the air or when they are "resuspended;" via eating contaminated food such as beef, eggs, milk, tea, mushrooms, seaweed, shellfish, and various fish; ingesting dust or soil, especially by children; and by "dermal contact."[159]

In studying dusts, Kaltofen looked for radioactive contamination in common dust collection areas such as air filters in cars and homes, shoes worn by children,

---

[158] web.archive.org/web/20160201221448/https://apha.confex.com/apha/139am/web program/Paper254015.html
[159] vimeo.com/33353060

house dust, topsoil, foods and plants. He also set up air sampling stations in Massachusetts, Boulder Colorado, Hawaii, San Francisco, Seattle, and various locations in Japan to see if he could find evidence of radioactive particles.

Although he didn't get into it, Kaltofen mentioned that at some point the "permissible radiation dose level" in the Fukushima area was officially raised to a whopping 20 times above the previously acceptable level...

Children's shoes laden with radioactivity
The results of the study were astonishing but not surprising. Dangerous radioactive particles were found in car filters. Children's shoes from Fukushima tested a whopping 166 times higher than normal, especially the soles and laces.[160]

Clean one day, radioactive the next
Eight months after the disaster, while airborne dust levels had dropped, soil levels were high, and "food chain radiation" was *increasing*. Equally disturbing, areas that had been "cleaned" could be re-contaminated by shifting radioactive dust. Surprisingly, about 93 miles away from Fukushima, near Tokyo, an "indoor home air filter was found with 230 Picocuries of radiation." For comparison, according to Kaltofen, the US limit for radiation in soil is 5 Picocuries.[161]

---

[160] web.archive.org/web/20160201221448/https://apha.confex.com/apha/139am/web program/Paper254015.

[161] web.archive.org/web/20160201221448/https://apha.confex.com/apha/139am/web program/Paper254015.html

Similar to our earlier discussion about radioactive zones, Kaltofen noted that the actual Japanese response to Fukushima by drawing circles around the hot zones and ascribing to them safety distances could be flawed since radioactive particles didn't just settle evenly and uniformly. Kaltofen noted that this meant, without proper testing, people in safer but closer areas might be evacuated to further but more dangerously contaminated areas... Add in that radioactive particles can become mobile via surface water and/or wind and you can see why continuous and proper testing is critical.

As to air samples in the US, Kaltofen's study found some radioactive particles in the air in both Boston and Seattle during the 2nd quarter of 2011. Kaltofen also noted that radioactive dust had been detected on the West Coast of the US, and specifically that Portland-area topsoil was found with up to 8,000 pCi/kg of cesium from Fukushima - which is apparently "over 10,000% higher than highest levels found by UC Berkeley."[162]

Black dust

In 2013, Kaltofen was interviewed about a sample of "black dust" from the restricted zone just outside the exclusion zone of Fukushima that he had recently analyzed. He explained that there had been for some time rumors of these larger *highly* radioactive black powder particles – found on streets and topsoil – in the Fukushima region, but this was the first sample he had been able to analyze.

---

[162] web.archive.org/web/20160219034350/http://enenews.com/university-researcher-topsoil-8000-pcikg-cesium-fukushima-10000-higher-highest-levels-found-uc-berkeley

After a series of tests, Kaltofen said that the particles weren't regular soil that had become contaminated but more of a black colored aggregation of radioactive particles – like "cheeseballs rolled in nuts" – "as if you took hundreds of very small radioactive particles and glued them together into different shapes and sizes."[163] And it proved to be highly radioactive.

While Kaltofen acknowledges that this black powder or dust sample may represent an extreme case because it is "strikingly concentrated and intense," he cautions that while possibly rare, the black dust is, unfortunately, not unique.[164]

Looking towards the future, Kaltofen feels the Fukushima contamination could be successfully addressed since "the technology and engineering is absolutely there to have an effective cleanup. All that has to happen is that people need to demand it and governments need to back up those demands..."[165]

A dollar and a dream... now, time for a tale about the fish that got away...

---

[163] fairewinds.org/nuclear-energy-education/japans-black-dust-with-marco-kaltofen

[164] fairewinds.org/nuclear-energy-education/japans-black-dust-with-marco-kaltofen

[165] fairewinds.org/nuclear-energy-education/japans-black-dust-with-marco-kaltofen

RADIOACTIVE FISH & KELP

"There is no safe level of radionuclide exposure, whether from food, water or other sources. Period."

— Jeff Paterson, DO
Former President
Physicians for Social Responsibility

Will radioactive contamination from the Fukushima disaster continue to foul the sea for decades?

In October 2012, in his article for *Science*, marine chemistry expert Ken O. Buesseler wrote that of the fish caught near Fukushima and then tested by the Japanese government, around 40% was still too contaminated to eat according to safety regulations established by the Japanese government. Buesseler stated that "The fact that many fish are just as contaminated today with cesium 134 and cesium 137 as they were more than one year ago implies that cesium is still being released into the food chain... (adding that with cesium's radioactivity lessening by half every 30 years) ...sediments would remain contaminated for decades to come."[166]

Decades to come...

---

[166] science.sciencemag.org/content/338/6106/480

Intrepid tuna

In May 2012 a radioactive Bluefin tuna made it 6,000 miles to the United States shoreline, startling scientists who didn't expect such large fish to retain radioactivity over such long journeys.

As CBS News reported "Five months after the Fukushima disaster... a team decided to test Pacific Bluefin that were caught off the coast of San Diego. To their surprise, tissue samples from all 15 tuna captured contained levels of two radioactive substances — ceisum-134 and cesium-137 — that were higher than in previous catches... the results 'are unequivocal. Fukushima was the source'..."

Stanford University noted in 2013 that "nearly two years after the (Fukushima) plant discharged radioactive materials into the ocean, follow-up research led by a biology PhD candidate at Stanford finds that young Pacific Bluefin tuna are still arriving in California carrying two of Fukushima's signature radioisotopes, cesium-134 and cesium-137."

South Korea and China play it safe

By September 2013, South Korea had banned the importing of any fish from the Fukushima region "in response to growing concern over the possible environmental impact of recent leaks of highly toxic water at the Fukushima Daiichi nuclear power plant...

"Despite assurances by Japan that it rigorously tests food for radiation, China has also maintained a ban on...

dairy, vegetable and seafood imports from several prefectures, including Fukushima, since March 2011."[167]

Nothing to concern yourself about

KUOW Puget Sound Public Radio noted in January 2014 that "Fisheries in Japan remain closed because of high levels of radioactivity and the ongoing release of contaminated groundwater from the nuclear site, but the FDA, Washington Department of Health, Woods Hole Oceanographic Institute and others have stressed that levels of radioactivity in fish that have made their way across the Pacific are not at levels of concern."[168]

In 2014, off the Oregon coast, albacore tuna tested by Oregon State University researchers revealed the fish were tainted with Fukushima radiation. "The study found detectable levels of Fukushima radiation in the 4-year-old fish. The majority of age 3 fish had no detectable level of Cesium-134. (A researcher)... said the amount found is very small compared to the radiation people are exposed to every day."[169]

Solitary salmon

In 2015, Snopes confirmed that a "salmon found in the Osoyoos Lake in British Columbia in 2015 had low but detectable levels of the radioactive isotope cesium-134, universally acknowledged as a marker for Fukushima radiation," but concluded that, "...the Fukushima disaster was a worldwide environmental catastrophe with global effects. The presence of a single North

---

[167] theguardian.com/world/2013/sep/06/south-korea-fish-japan-fukushima
[168] earthfix.opb.org/water/article/scientists-say-stop-worrying-about-fukushima-radio/
169earthfix.opb.org/flora-and-fauna/article/researchers-detect-fukushima-radiation-in-albacore

American salmon with trace levels of cesium-134, undoubtedly the result of the Fukushima event, will nevertheless have a barely negligible – let alone catastrophic – effect on public health."[170]

Kelp

University of California Berkeley's *Kelp Watch 2015* monitored radioactivity in kelp and "started as California centric but has continued to grow beyond the California coastline and includes locations in Baja-Mexico, Oregon, Washington, British Columbia and Alaska..." It was discontinued after 2016 since "there was no indication that the radioactivity from Fukushima became incorporated in the coastal kelp beds sampled."[171]

Bottom-feeders

In the mid-2016 study *Fukushima Daiichi–Derived Radionuclides in the Ocean: Transport, Fate, and Impacts* researchers noted that "...by October 2012, TEPCO had reported extremely high Cs (radioactive cesium) activities – up to thousands of becquerels per kilogram wet weight in various demersal (living near the bottom of the sea) species sampled in the (Fukushima) harbor. Some fish caught within the harbor remain highly contaminated even 5 years after the accident and are now prevented from leaving the contaminated area by a net."[172] *Highly contaminated 5 years later...*

---

[170] snopes.com/fact-check/radioactive-salmon-fukushima/

[171] kelpwatch.berkeley.edu/Home

[172] Fukushima Daiichi–Derived Radionuclides in the Ocean: Transport, Fate, and Impacts ; Ken Buesseler, Minhan Dai, Michio Aoyama, Claudia Benitez-Nelson, Sabine Charmasson, Kathryn Higley, Vladimir Maderich, Pere Masqué, Paul J. Morris, Deborah Oughton, John N. Smith; Annual Review of Marine Science 2017 9:1, 173-203

EU eases, others don't

By 2016, the European Union "began easing its own restrictions on Japanese imports in 2016... (but) China, Taiwan, Hong Kong, Macao, Singapore and Russia all continued to ban products from certain (Japanese) regions."[173] *What do they know?*

Kelp decline

In 2018 the Monterey Herald reported that since 2015 kelp "has declined by as much as 95 percent along the Northern California coastline..."

The cause? "Above average water temperature and an increase in sea urchin populations..."

Not a whisper of radiation.

The effect? "The loss of this annual alga has had significant effects on other marine species, many of which rely on these forests for shelter and food..."[174]

Sure enough, by 2017 researchers noticed that abalone (sea snails) were starving to death and there was "a 65% reduction in abalone density compared with populations from a decade before..."[175] so California closed off the area hoping divers that fish for abalone switch to other marine life to harvest...

And, of course, there is no guarantee if and when the kelp will return...

---

[173] ibtimes.com/fukushima-japan-ban-fish-exports-over-after-nuclear-radiation-disaster-countries-2508805
[174] montereyherald.com/2018/02/01/earth-matters-the-loss-of-our-kelp-forests/
[175] montereyherald.com/2018/02/01/earth-matters-the-loss-of-our-kelp-forests/

RADIOACTIVE INSECTS

"If we were to wipe out insects alone on this planet, the rest of life and humanity with it would mostly disappear from the land. Within a few months.

— E.O. Wilson

Science reported in 2014 that radiation from Fukushima was still causing problems. Initially "local wildlife were exposed both externally to radiation in the environment and internally from contaminated food sources."[176]

Specifically studying butterflies, Japanese scientists had found that "Larvae that dined on the radiation-drenched leaves had low survival rates and high incidences of physical abnormalities such as unusually small forewings. These results corroborated field surveys by others that turned up fewer butterflies in contaminated areas than would normally be expected..."[177]

In a new study Japanese researchers found that even "low-dose ingestion... may be seriously toxic to certain organisms."[178]

---

[176] sciencemag.org/news/2014/09/fukushima-radiation-still-poisoning-insects

[177] sciencemag.org/news/2014/09/fukushima-radiation-still-poisoning-insects

[178] sciencemag.org/news/2014/09/fukushima-radiation-still-poisoning-insects

Further, they discovered that "Larvae fed the contaminated leaves had even lower survival rates and more abnormalities than their parents"[179] that had also eaten the contaminated leaves.

In Science Daily, readers learned in 2014 that studies were revealing that there were serious biological consequences to plants and animals. "A growing body of empirical results from studies of birds, monkeys, butterflies, and other insects suggests that some species have been significantly impacted by the radioactive releases related to the Fukushima disaster," stated Dr. Timothy Mousseau of the University of South Carolina, lead author of one of the studies."[180]

Radiation catches up to animals
Also in 2014, the American Genetic Association reported that "Population censuses of birds, butterflies, and cicadas at Fukushima showed major declines attributable to radiation exposure. Morphological effects, such as aberrant feathers on barn swallows, were also observed..."[181]

So what's the big deal? I hate creepy crawlers, squirming bugs, biting insects... so what if they all die off?

Actually a matter of life and death. Literally. Insects are a critical part of the food chain. They pollinate all sorts of plants. They decompose soil keeping it healthy. And more...

____

[179] sciencemag.org/news/2014/09/fukushima-radiation-still-poisoning-insects
[180] sciencedaily.com/releases/2014/08/140814124535.htm
[181] phys.org/news/2014-08-biological-effects-fukushima-insects-animals.html

Insects make the world go 'round

The Washington Post quoted an environmentalist in October 2017 explaining that "if you like to eat nutritious fruits and vegetables, you should thank an insect. If you like salmon, you can thank a tiny fly that the salmon eat when they're young... The whole fabric of our planet is built on plants and insects and the relationship between the two."[182]

Armageddon 2017

In October 2017, the BBC reported that although the causes are unknown, "scientists have long suspected that insects are in dramatic decline, but new evidence confirms this... The loss of insects has far-reaching consequences for entire ecosystems... Insects provide a food source for many birds, amphibians, bats and reptiles, while plants rely on insects for pollination... The decline is more severe than found in previous studies..."[183]

Reacting to similar evidence, RT called it the "Ecological Armageddon" that "could ravage life on Earth" and explained that "insects are essential for life on Earth as they act as pollinators and prey for other species."[184]

Apocalypse 2018

Near the end of 2018, The New York Times featured a disturbing story "The Insect Apocalypse is Here," reported on the shocking loss of insects across many species, and asked a scientist what an insect-less world

---

[182] washingtonpost.com/news/speaking-of-science/wp/2017/10/18/this-is-very-alarming-flying-insects-vanish-from-nature-preserves/

[183] bbc.com/news/science-environment-41670472

[184] rt.com/news/407215-insect-population-decline-study/

would look like. He described "a flowerless world with silent forests, a world of dung and old leaves and rotting carcasses accumulating in cities and roadsides, a world of 'collapse or decay and erosion and loss that would spread through ecosystems' – spiraling from predators to plants..."[185] *Charming...*

But why is it happening?
Remember all those dead rotting fish and other massive die-offs from a previous chapter? And how there were often few definitive reasons given to explain what was happening? Prepare for déjà vu...

As to causes for the insect decimation, the answers range from "no one knows" to "increased urbanization, habitat loss and pesticide use."[186] Ok. But did you notice again what's missing? *Setting aside chemtrails or 5G...*

Has there been any real scientific investigation into whether airborne radiation from the Fukushima disaster might have contributed to insect decimation? We couldn't find anything... Why is that?

All anyone "knows" is that it will be bad... As famed biologist E.O. Wilson noted, "If all mankind were to disappear, the world would regenerate back to the rich state of equilibrium that existed ten thousand years ago. If insects were to vanish, the environment would collapse into chaos."

Poof. Gone... Maybe all that will be left will be wild dangerous sharp-toothed wild boars...

---

[185] nytimes.com/2018/11/27/magazine/insect-apocalypse.html
[186] rt.com/news/407215-insect-population-decline-study/

RADIOACTIVE WILD BOARS

"I wish for the day to come when we can eat wild game again."

Hidekiyo Tachiya
Mayor of Soma near Fukushima[187]

Many in Northern Japan enjoy dining on wild boar and consider the meat a delicacy. *Or they used to...*

Residents trying to return to their neighborhoods six years after mandatory evacuations of communities near the Fukushima meltdown were greeted by unexpected new residents... wild boars.

Cool! Organize a hunt and set a world record for the largest wild boar BBQ ever, right?

Not exactly.

That wild boars freely roam the streets near Fukushima is bad enough. Many have lost the fear of humans, and boars can be super dangerous. Worse, quite a few have taken up residence in homes and buildings abandoned after the nuclear disaster.

---

[187] nytimes.com/2017/03/09/world/asia/radioactive-boars-in-fukushima-thwart-residents-plans-to-return-home.html

But *far worse* is that these boars are positively "glowing." According to a March 9, 2017, New York Times story, *Radioactive Boars in Fukushima Thwart Residents' Plans to Return Home*, some boars tested by the Japanese government "have shown levels of radioactive element cesium-137 that are 300 times higher than safety standards."[188]

300 times higher than safety standards. Dang!

Open season on glowing boars

Back to the hunting idea but with a twist... Reuters reported on March 8, 2017, that "hundreds of radioactive wild boars"[189] were running loose in towns near the Fukushima plant. With boars destroying local farms, gorging on radioactive plants, and occasionally attacking people, the government hired hunters to get rid of the toxic beasts.

And it's not just a few hundred boars... "The latest statistics show that in the three years since 2014, the number of boars killed in hunts has grown to 13,000 from 3,000."[190] Imagine the pain hunters must develop in their trigger fingers alone... 13,000...

Where to dump all these carcasses has become a problem as local municipalities say they're running out of land. Some boars are being buried in mass pits,

---

[188] nytimes.com/2017/03/09/world/asia/radioactive-boars-in-fukushima-thwart-residents-plans-to-return-home.html

[189] reuters.com/video/2017/03/09/fukushima-hit-towns-scramble-to-clear-ou?videoId=371268563

[190] nytimes.com/2017/03/09/world/asia/radioactive-boars-in-fukushima-thwart-residents-plans-to-return-home.html

others are being incinerated. Anyone want to guess what's happening to all the radioactivity?

It also seems that in the six short years since people evacuated the surrounding area, beyond boars, other animals have moved in as well. Legions of rats have commandeered supermarkets, mangy dogs roam the streets, and foxes frolic in the grasslands.

Dedicated to repopulating their towns, local officials came up with many creative suggestions on battling the wild boar invasion such as custom-made boar traps and scaring away boars with drones...

Yeah. Ok.

It's no wonder that over half of the former residents of Fukushima told the government "they wouldn't return, citing fears over radiation and the safety of the nuclear plant, which will take 40 years to dismantle."[191]

I'll drink to that. Maybe...

---

[191] nytimes.com/2017/03/09/world/asia/radioactive-boars-in-fukushima-thwart-residents-plans-to-return-home.html

RADIOACTIVE WINE

"Here's to wine, wit and wisdom – wine enough to sharpen wit; wit enough to give zest to wine and wisdom enough to know when we have had enough."

— 20th Century Book of Toasts
(David McKay 1910)

The Weather Channel reported on July 23, 2018, that the radioactive cloud from the Fukushima disaster "spread to other parts of the world" including, apparently, to wineries in California.[192]

When scientists tested some wines produced in California after the Fukushima event, sure enough, they found miniscule levels of "cesium-137 signatures that could be traced back to the disaster…"[193]

The scientists from the University of Bordeaux noted in their report that "In January 2017, we came across a series of Californian wines… from vintage 2009 to 2012. The Fukushima incident, which took place on March 11, 2011, resulted in a radioactive cloud that has crossed the Pacific Ocean to reach the west coast of the United

---

[192] weather.com/science/environment/video/fukushima-nuclear-signature-detected-in-california-wines

[193] weather.com/science/environment/video/fukushima-nuclear-signature-detected-in-california-wines

States. And in Northern California, there is the Nappa Valley. The idea was then to see if, as is the case in Europe following the Chernobyl accident, we could detect a variation in the cesium-137 level in these wines."[194]

After testing, the scientists reported they found "an increase in activity in 2011 by a factor of 2..."[195]

On July 20, 2018, according to The New York Times, the levels found by the scientists were "much higher than the usual level... (and that) ingesting cesium-137 can result in an elevated risk for cancer, but the level of radioactive material from Fukushima in food and drink in countries outside Japan has been too low to result in a health hazard, according to the World Health Organization."[196]

That's kind of cool. Like you can literally internulize some of Fukushima without having to travel there...

---

[194] arxiv.org/ftp/arxiv/papers/1807/1807.04340.pdf

[195] arxiv.org/ftp/arxiv/papers/1807/1807.04340.pdf

[196] nytimes.com/2018/07/20/science/fukushima-radiation-levels-california-wine-nyt.html

RADIOACTIVE TRAVEL

"Nuclear Tourism will let you take the radiation back home after your holiday has ended."

—Anthony T. Hincks

In late 2010, comedian Conan O'Brien famously quipped, "Ukraine announced plans to open Chernobyl, their nuclear disaster site, to tourists. They say it's just like Disneyland, except the 6-foot mouse is real."

And it was no joke that the Ukraine had decided to actively promote tourism to the disaster site. "While the area remains heavily contaminated, a ministry spokeswoman said, tourism routes had been drawn up which would cover the main sights while steering clear of the dangerous spots. Wandering would not be encouraged, Yulia Yurshova said: 'There are things to see there if one follows the official route and doesn't stray away from the group.'"[197] Yurshova also told The Wall Street Journal the Ukraine wants to "work with big tour operators and attract Western tourists, from whom there's great demand."[198]

Someone in Japan apparently was paying close attention.

---

[197] theguardian.com/world/2010/dec/13/chernobyl-now-open-to-tourists
[198] wsj.com/articles/SB10001424052748703727804576017720342095028

In late summer 2017, saying he would like "Vietnamese people to see Fukushima making its way on reconstruction" and to "feel hope for the future," the ever-resourceful governor of Fukushima made a bombshell announcement... apparently he had convinced a travel agency and an airline in Viet Nam to create special packages for tourists to showcase Fukushima. Seriously.

For a quarter of a year in 2018, the goal was to increase flights and tourists from Ho Chi Minh City to Fukushima to help boost the economy and to show off progress.

The pears taste great
Not yet finished, as part of the promotion the Governor apparently convinced a local supermarket in Ho Chi Minh City to sell pears grown in Fukushima. According to the Japan Times, "when Vietnamese told him the Fukushima pears were delicious... (the Governor) felt confident about eliminating unfounded rumors that food from Fukushima is contaminated with fallout from the core meltdowns at the Fukushima No. 1 power plant..."[199]

You really can't make this stuff up...

But wait. There's more...

Billing itself as a "life-changing tour," the Knot World travel agency arranges for tours of the Fukushima disaster area so travelers can "know and feel FUKUSHIMA one step deeper..."

---

[199] japantimes.co.jp/news/2017/08/26/national/vietnamese-increase-charter-flights-fukushima/

Life-changing no doubt... So where exactly will you and your fellow travelers wander and roam to know and feel the disaster deeper?

According to the travel agency you'll "Visit the area within 20 km of Fukushima Daiichi Nuclear Power Plant and see the Fukushima disaster zone with your own eyes."[200] The one-day 12-hour tour (with 5 hours in Fukushima) is broken down into three sections: past, present, and future.

- The *past* has visitors by the coast to see where the tsunami hit.

- The *future* part of the tour involves areas where people are rebuilding with a sense of hope.

- The *present* has tourists, "Visiting the area where people are not allowed to live because the radiation is so high. This (according to the tour operators) will help you understand how terrible the situation is..."[201]

Or maybe you and your significant loved ones would prefer the official Japanese-government-sponsored tour *Real Fukushima* where you can spend 4-5 hours exploring the sites. But just remember "you are not allowed to enter red zone, but you can pass through it on designated roads..." And don't worry! A dose meter is loaned to you so you can enjoy monitoring yourself since "the total amount of the radiation exposure through the tour is around 3-5 micro Sievert."[202]

---

[200] fukushima.tohoku-tour.com/

[201] japanwondertravel.com/products/fukushima-disaster-area-day-tour-from-tokyo-within-20-km-of-fukushima-nuclear-power-plant

[202] real-fukushima.com/

RADIOACTIVE BUCKYBALLS

> "What the hell is a buckyball?"
> —Our editor

Buckyballs look like tiny soccer balls. They were created when the Japanese used tons of sea and fresh water to cool down the Fukushima reactors that were melting.

When the water hit the "incredibly hot and radioactive, primarily uranium-oxide fuel (it) turns it into peroxide. In this goo mix, buckyballs are formed, loaded with uranium and able to move quickly through water without disintegrating."[203]

Surfing buckyballs

As reported in *See California*, data from the EPA, "combined with the UC Davis study of buckyballs and a European study of sea spray radiation spread, strongly indicate that Southern California is being exposed to significant amounts of radiation. The closer to the coast, the more pronounced the radiation in this scenario... The main wave of water-borne radiation from the meltdowns, including highly mobile uranium-60 buckyballs, is surging across the Pacific along the Kuroshio Current, second only to the Gulf Stream for power on the planet..."[204]

---

[203] seecalifornia.com/news/fukushima-disaster-and-its-global-reach/

[204] seecalifornia.com/news/fukushima-disaster-and-its-global-reach/

Environmental journalist Michael Collins reported in July 2012 that a "UK study found that the Irish Sea has a micro layer on top of it... that can become imbued with fine particulate material and its absorbed radiation. These concentrations of plutonium and americium are four to five times their concentrations in ambient seawater. Plutonium concentrates by 26,000 times in floating algal blooms at sea, says the report. These radionuclides and buckyballs make up the goo inexorably crossing the Pacific, which may just have begun to impact our shores."[205] Great. Just great...

Like a bad dream children might have...

---

[205] enviroreporter.com/author/michael-collins/

RADIOACTIVE CHILDREN

"Children are much more susceptible to the effects of radiation, and stand a much greater chance of developing cancer than adults. So it is particularly dangerous when they consume radioactive food or water."

Dr. Andrew Kanter
President of the Board
Physicians for Social Responsibility

In April 2011, The Asia-Pacific Journal asked the mayor of Minami-Soma, a Fukushima prefecture, to address health risks amidst schools reopening in the region. The mayor made some very influential statements the gist of which seemed to be that *local radiation levels are not that dangerous...*

"Regardless of the radiation problem, cancer rates are already surging in society and we need to address this issue realistically."

"No one even knows for sure how many people died as a result of the Chernobyl disaster—it's as if people are afraid of a ghost that never appears."

"I don't want to incite fear among the people."[206]

---

[206] apjjf.org/-Makiko-Segawa/3516/article.pdf

Just exaggerations

The Asia-Pacific Journal also quoted the president of a local sewage business who said, "There is no worry about radiation here; it's just an exaggeration."[207]

The article ended with a local mother complaining that an officer with the Self-Defense Forces assigned to the area "refused to answer her question when she asked how much radiation they were detecting in the area. The officer said that he was under orders not to give out such information to the local residents."[208]

Lack of trust

In any case, the mother told the media that she didn't trust the Japanese government, and that no amount of reported radiation, or monetary compensation, would sway her to leave her family home...

Radioactive rides

Writing on the Fukushima Voice blog, a contributor recounted her personal experience. Identifying as a registered nurse, the poster detailed how she believes her twin nephews were exposed to radiation from numerous rides they took in a car that had been thought to be "decontaminated."[209]

The nurse recounts that after the previously healthy twins began to exhibit many debilitating symptoms of radiation poisoning, lab tests revealed dangerously high

---

[207] apjjf.org/-Makiko-Segawa/3516/article.pdf

[208] apjjf.org/-Makiko-Segawa/3516/article.pdf

[209] fukushimavoice-eng.blogspot.com/2012/01/from-hokkaido-twins-that-got-radiation.html

levels of radiation in the car. She also provides links to photos, certificates, and doctor's reports.

The father of the affected twins has a website as well where he begs the Japanese people to talk openly about radiation and to take precautionary measures wherever possible while advocating for protecting children's health.[210]

He cautioned,

"This problem is not limited to my children. There may be tens of thousands, or even hundreds of thousands of contaminated cars operated all over Japan. Unless we immediately stop them, there would be more children exposed to radiation. The twins, through radiation exposure (probably through inhalation) developed such symptoms as fatigue, lethargy, twitching, walking difficulty, muscle pain and muscle atrophy, but not everyone develops the same symptoms… Unless you recognize the facts of radioactive contamination, you will only receive an ordinary, routine diagnosis of colds or something like that, and you will be given usual medications, when you or your children develop some symptoms. It is extremely difficult to assess individually whether the symptoms are due to radiation. It's not until one year, or five, ten, or twenty years later, when there is enough statistical data available that they might say that it might be due to radiation. Do you want your child to be just one of the statistical numbers?"[211]

---

[210] 2011kazu.web.fc2.com/

[211] fukushimavoice-eng.blogspot.com/2012/01/from-hokkaido-twins-that-got-radiation.html

Cancer spike but no worries

Something weird was happening. ABC (Australia) reported in March 2015 that "Before the disaster, there was just one to two cases of thyroid cancers in a million Japanese children but now Fukushima has more than 100 confirmed or suspected cases, having tested about 300,000 children."[212]

No need to worry according to some scientists and the United Nations who opined that these heightened results were likely due to "doing more testing with more sensitive equipment..."[213]

Kind of like saying, *you'll find what you look for...*

It takes a while

It is thought that thyroid cancer has the potential to "turn up about four to five years after a nuclear disaster... In Chernobyl about 6,000 children contracted thyroid cancer..."[214]

All in all, many people were concerned that decontamination and testing were less than thorough...

In October 2015, NPR reported that although apologists where busy shrugging off claims of elevated thyroid cancer in the Fukushima region and pointing at poor study methods and "increased vigilance" (*if you seek it vigilantly you shall find it*), research done at Okayama

---

[212] abc.net.au/news/2015-03-11/fukushima-radiation-levels-high-four-years-after-disaster/6297718

[213] abc.net.au/news/2015-03-11/fukushima-radiation-levels-high-four-years-after-disaster/6297718

[214] abc.net.au/news/2015-03-11/fukushima-radiation-levels-high-four-years-after-disaster/6297718

University specifically concluded that "the increase in cancer is 'unlikely to be caused by a screening surge,' and that thyroid cancer rates are highly elevated throughout Fukushima..."[215]

Better not to talk about it

Around the same time, the Japan Times published a story explaining that with much contradictory information about Fukushima region cancer rates and the effects of radiation, "In accordance with the official line regarding the possible health crisis in Fukushima, it's better not to talk about it at all... This attitude only exacerbates the situation... residents don't trust anyone representing the authorities to give them straight answers..."[216]

Warning from a survivor

In the summer of 2016, CBS News reported about a 21-year-old Japanese girl from the Fukushima region who had developed thyroid cancer.

Since speaking about cancer and Fukushima seems to somehow be politically incorrect, and getting screened for cancer wasn't getting air-time, the girl made a plea to everyone in the region to get screened. "'There aren't many people like me who will openly speak out,' said the young woman, who requested anonymity because of fears about harassment... I want everyone, all the children, to go to the hospital and get screened. They think it's too much trouble, and there are no risks, and

---

[215] npr.org/sections/thetwo-way/2015/10/08/446873871/fukushima-study-links-childrens-cancer-to-nuclear-accident

[216] japantimes.co.jp/news/2015/10/31/national/media-national/cancer-fukushima-trust/

they don't go... My cancer was detected early, and I learned that was important.'"[217]

Early detection is important for sure since according to the American Thyroid Association, "Even when thyroid cancer is more advanced, effective treatment is available for the most common forms of thyroid cancer. Even though the diagnosis of cancer is terrifying, the prognosis for most patients with papillary and follicular thyroid cancer is usually excellent..."[218]

So, Fukushima, get screened. And tell everyone you know to get screened...

Stigmatizing the victims of radiation
A local Fukushima photographer said people fear discussing radiation exposure and cancer, and summed up the issue saying, "They feel alone. They can't even tell their relatives... They feel they can't tell anyone. They felt they were not allowed to ask questions."[219]

Imagine how bad it must be to have radiation illness, or cancer, or anything related... or to suspect that you might be sick... and to have to *hide* your illness because of some sort of shaming or twisted "social norms."

It is 2019... illness is NOT a stigma. *No matter what,* illness is not a stigma. Especially when those that are ill were victims of a nuclear disaster... So, Fukushima, get screened. And tell everyone you know to get screened...

---

[217] cbsnews.com/news/japan-fukushima-thyroid-cancer-patient-is-first-to-speak-out/
[218] thyroid.org/thyroid-cancer/
[219] cbsnews.com/news/japan-fukushima-thyroid-cancer-patient-is-first-to-speak-out/

Now, on to children eating healthy meals... Following is a story which is either a complete innocent coincidence, or is so dark that it defies any sane explanation...

Glowing school lunches?

On March 19, 2013, Japan Today broke a story about a contractor that was providing school lunches for junior high school in Tokyo's Komae City. Mysteriously, within days of the City announcing it would be testing lunch ingredients for radioactivity, the contractor announced they would not renew their contract even though the School Lunch Act calls for a 6 months' notice...

With no time "to find a suitable replacement," about "1,050 students and teachers" were on their own... "The Education Ministry said having a school unable to serve lunch was an exceptionally rare occurrence."[220]

One can only wonder what that food contractor thought the radiation tests might reveal...

New national crisis

Birthrates in Japan were gradually declining over the years, but after Fukushima they "fell off a cliff."[221] Japan's Prime Minister identified falling birthrates as a new "national crisis" in Japan in 2018 – Japan suffered "its biggest population decline on record... (and) the number of births fell to its lowest since records began more than a century ago..."[222]

---

[220] japantoday.com/category/national/contractor-refuses-to-provide-school-lunches-when-faced-with-radiation-checks

[221] nuclear-news.net/2019/01/07/the-after-fukushima-and-japans-declining-birthrate-japans-demographics-a-national-crisis/

[222] irishtimes.com/news/world/asia-pacific/japan-suffers-biggest-ever-population-decline-as-birthrate-falls-

MILLIONS OF TONS OF DEBRIS

"You can't cross the sea merely by standing and staring
at the water."

— Rabindranath Tagore

We take a quick break from all the radioactivity to remember that just before the nuclear disaster, there was the tsunami disaster. Loads of debris, from tiny to gigantic, was swept out to sea. Much is still there. It may not be radioactive, but it can be hazardous...

In March 2012, the BBC reported that an empty Japanese fishing ship was spotted drifting towards Canada and was "believed to be the first large item from the millions of tons of tsunami debris to cross the Pacific... The main mass of the debris is not expected to make landfall in North America until March 2014." [223]

According to University of Hawaii researchers, the tsunami "generated more than 25 million tons of debris... Between 4 and 8 million tons were washed into the ocean, with 1 to 2 million tons still floating on the surface..."[224]

---

[223] bbc.com/news/world-us-canada-17500008
[224] bbc.com/news/world-us-canada-17500008

May 2012 saw residents of Alaska concerned about all the debris washing up on its islands and shores. A CBS reporter on the scene noted that "at the mouth of Prince William Sound, there are bottles and barrels, spray cans, fishing gear and worries about toxic chemicals. The Japanese writing on this fuel canister says 'Danger.'"[225] And of course the vast amount of Styrofoam and plastic waste can really screw up the environment as well as kill wildlife and fish...

A marine debris director from NOAA explained that "the Fukushima plant had a meltdown after the debris was already in the water. And from the experts we've talked to about radiation, they think that the isotopes would be weathered and be gone because of their half-lives by now..."[226]

Hmmm...

In July 2013, a crew of sailors in the Pacific was angling to set a world record in a 73-foot yacht considered one of the fastest in the world. While they won the 2,560 mile race, they were slowed down significantly as they had to deal with massive amounts of Fukushima debris.

"'We experienced 'Fukushima's Revenge' (reported the yacht owner)... his boat sustained significant damage after hitting two telephone poles and other objects..."[227]

It's like Fukushima tried to rain on his parade...

---

[225] cbsnews.com/news/toxic-japanese-debris-piles-up-on-alaskas-shore/

[226] cbsnews.com/news/toxic-japanese-debris-piles-up-on-alaskas-shore/

[227] cnn.com/2013/07/19/us/hawaii-sailrace-record/index.html

RADIOACTIVE RAIN

"Fukushima fallout appeared to affect all areas of the U.S., and was especially large in some, mostly in the western part of the nation."

Joseph J. Mangano & Janette D. Sherman

Remember Arnie Gundersen from a previous chapter? It's not just food imported from Japan that has him worried.

Gundersen is convinced that the effects of Fukushima are far from over... Beyond his revealing that Hillary Clinton knowingly agreed with the Japanese officials to keep importing food without proper testing, Gundersen believes that radioactive water is still leaking into the ocean and knows that it's leaking into the ground table.

Well, the Japanese can simply contain the radioactive waste to one area, right? And then clean it up. Right??

Probably, if they didn't send it up into the air...

Gundersen says that the Japanese are actually burning radioactive waste in order to get rid of it...

You mean like people used to do with piles of leaves in the Fall? But isn't nuclear waste a special kind of resilient?

According to the Institute for Energy and Environmental Research, "Incineration does not destroy metals or reduce radioactivity of wastes. Radioactive waste incinerators… can capture all but a small fraction of the radioactive isotopes and metals fed into them. The fraction that does escape, however, tends to be in the form of small particles that are more readily absorbed by living organisms than larger particles."[228]

Gundersen says that straw fed to livestock as well as rice harvested for human consumption is at serious risk for being contaminated. And passing that contamination along, on and on…

Oh, and if that isn't scary enough, the incineration also usually creates "toxic by-products… (that) can be more toxic per unit weight than the original wastes… (which) accumulate in fatty tissue, increasing in concentration at each successive level of the food chain…"[229]

Dang!

Spreading waste

Burning only serves to spread the waste, Gundersen says, because as it "burns" it really just gets airborne and moves to adjacent areas… and those areas detect the radiation and burn the newly contaminated materials which sends the radiation airborne again… and so on and so on… to the point that Gundersen fully expects the radiation to potentially end up in Hawaii

---

[228] ieer.org/resource/factsheets/incineration-radioactive-mixed/

[229] ieer.org/resource/factsheets/incineration-radioactive-mixed/

and/or on the West Coast of the United States and Canada.[230]

Rethinking dancing in the rain

Gundersen also worries about "rain-outs" which is explained by Harvard and Stanford educated political scientist, lawyer, and Columbia University faculty member Tonya Putnam, as "...rain washing radioactive materials from the atmosphere onto the ground."[231]

Think about that the next time you're out for a stroll in the rain...

Guessing that burning radioactive waste and sending it into the sky via smoke clouds only to have it rain down on the people, plants, soil, animals, etc. etc. is just not going to end well...

Worse than previously thought

That was in 2011. By Summer 2017, Gundersen's Fairewinds Energy Foundation issued a press release noting a new scientific study showed that "Full Radiation Risks are not Recorded"[232] and that "based on 415 samples of radioactive dust from Japan, the USA, and Canada, the study identified a statistically meaningful number of samples that were considerably more radioactive than current radiation models anticipated. If ingested, these more radioactive particles

---

[230] web.archive.org/web/20120127150635/http://www.solarimg.org/shows/SolarIMG_podcast_Arnie_Gundersen_130811.mp3
[231] web.archive.org/web/20070610233310/http://iis-db.stanford.edu/pubs/20063/NuclearRisk.pdf
[232] fairewinds.org/newsletter-archive//press-release-radioactively-hot-particles-in-japan

increase the risk of suffering a future health problem."[233]

The study also found that "some people were breathing or ingesting enough radioactive dust to have a real increase in their risk of suffering a future health problem. This was especially true of children and younger people, who inhale or ingest proportionately more dust than adults."[234]

Radioactive rain in US

In 2013, Radiation and Public Health Project researchers out of New York released a report titled "Elevated airborne beta levels in Pacific/West Coast US States and trends in hypothyroidism among newborns after the Fukushima nuclear meltdown." It was published in the *Open Journal of Pediatrics* and said that "Large amounts of fallout disseminated worldwide from the meltdowns in... the Fukushima-Daiichi plant... included radioiodine isotopes. Just days after the meltdowns, I-131 (radioactive iodine from Fukushima) concentrations in US precipitation was measured up to 211 times above normal."[235]

Hyperthyroidism spike in US newborns

The study followed children born in Alaska, California, Hawaii, Oregon, and Washington from 1-16 weeks after the Fukushima disaster. They were compared to various other US states and found that "The number of congenital hypothyroid cases in these five states from March 17-December 31, 2011 was 16% greater than for

---

[233] fairewinds.org/newsletter-archive//press-release-radioactively-hot-particles-in-japan

[234] fairewinds.org/newsletter-archive//press-release-radioactively-hot-particles-in-japan

[235] scirp.org/journal/PaperInformation.aspx?PaperID=28599

the same period in 2010, compared to a 3% decline in 36 other US States."[236]

Researchers also noted that "Young children born in the United States West Coast, right in the line of fire for radioactive isotopes, have been found to be 28 percent more likely to develop congenital hypothyroidism than infants born the year before the incident."[237]

So surely the mainstream media was all over it... *Not.*

Luckily, *solely for them*, many politicians and members of the mainstream media are either literal dimwits or live in an alternate reality, and they seem to sincerely, or recklessly, believe that nuclear radiation simply doesn't apply to them, let alone pose any real danger ...

And there are platoons of people eager and willing to explain away anything and everything.

Cue the apologists...

---

[236] file.scirp.org/Html/1-1330150_28599.htm

[237] integrativecanceranswers.com/fukushima-nuclear-disaster-increased-thyroid-cancer-in-u-s/

RADIOACTIVE APOLOGISTS

"...a dozen years back during the invasion of Iraq when the helicopter we were traveling in was forced down after being hit by an RPG."

— Brian Williams
Former NBC News anchor who fabricated a story about being in a helicopter that Iraqi forces shot

Shortly after the Fukushima disaster, quite a few efforts to quell fear and calm down the masses sprang to life. And the radioactivity apologists weren't just from the Japanese government. People from all over grabbed headlines with tales of *nothing to worry about.*

After all, *everything* is radioactive.

Bananas and bricks!
In May 2011, a radiation epidemiologist, Professor in the Department of Medicine at Vanderbilt University, Scientific Director of the International Epidemiology Institute, Commissioner of the International Commission on Radiological Protection, an emeritus member of the National Council on Radiation Protection and Measurements, a U.S. delegate to the United Nations Scientific Committee on the Effects of Atomic Radiation, and a member of the Congressionally-mandated Veterans Advisory Board on Dose Reconstruction who

spent his career studying people exposed to radiation testified before Congress…

His testimony revealed *his belief* that:
- Fukushima is not Chernobyl
- The health consequences for Japanese workers and public appear to be minor
- The health consequences for United States citizens are negligible to nonexistent.
- We live in a radioactive world
- There is a pressing need to learn more about the health consequences of radiation

He also admonished fearmongers by noting that, "To place the radiation levels from Fukushima in brief perspective, it is important to recognize that we live in a radioactive world.

"A banana, for example, has 10 Bq of activity…

"All the foodstuffs we eat that contain potassium also contain a small amount of radioactive potassium, a primordial element with a billion year half-life. There are no concerns and no health consequences from such exposures.

"We breathe radioactive radon which contributes over the year to about 210 millirem of natural background radiation. (1 millirem = 10 microsieverts.[238])

"Bricks and granite contain radioactive materials that result in radiation exposures to the public - 20 millirem.

---

[238] easysurf.cc/cnver24.htm#mrmtomcsv5

"The Capitol Building was constructed with granite and is frequently cited as having some of the highest radiation levels in all of the United States, about 85 millirem per year.

"Water contains small amounts of radioactive radium, thorium and uranium, all within allowable limits.

"Not only do we live in a radioactive world, our bodies are radioactive (30 millirem per year). Each second over 7,000 radioactive atoms in our bodies decay and can irradiate those sitting next to us. The atoms are largely radioactive potassium in our muscles and carbon-14 in our tissues.

"The amount of radiation we receive each year from medical sources (300 millirem), such as CT and medical imaging, equals the amount received from natural sources (300 millirem).

"International travel increases our exposure to cosmic rays and space radiation. A roundtrip from Dulles to Tokyo would result in 20 millirem.

"Living in Denver for a year results in 450 millirem of radiation dose, or 35% more than the U.S. average of 310 millirem from natural sources.

"About 2.5 million Americans (0.8% of the population) receive more than 2,000 millirem per year from natural sources.

"These examples are not to minimize the health consequences of high-level exposures which are clearly demonstrable in human populations and include acute radiation sickness at very high doses in excess of 200 rem and an increase in cancer at moderate doses above about 10 rem (10,000 millirem). The examples do indicate, however, that we live in a world of 7 low-level radiation for which the possible health consequences are of little concern.

"The exposures to the U.S. population from Fukushima are tiny and thousands of times below U.S. standards or guidelines where remedial action would be triggered."[239]

He concluded that "The lasting effects upon the Japanese population will most likely be psychological with increased occurrence of stress-related mental disorders and depression associated not necessarily with the concern about reactor radiation, but with the horrific loss of life and disruption caused by the tsunami and earthquake."[240]

Oh. Ok. So that was the tone in 2011...

Seek and you shall find redux

In March of 2016, Wired magazine ran a story titled *Cancer Rates Spiked After Fukushima. But Don't Blame Radiation.* The article concluded with "So, will the kids who lived near the Fukushima plant suffer more thyroid cancer than their peers elsewhere? Well, yes. Probably. They are going to be screened more than most other kids, after all, and those screenings will turn up more thyroid cancer, just by virtue of the fact that people are looking for it." [241]

---

239 hps.org/documents/John_Boice_Testimony_13_May_2011.pdf
240 hps.org/documents/John_Boice_Testimony_13_May_2011.pdf
241 wired.com/2016/03/cancer-rates-spiked-fukushima-dont-blame-radiation/

Really? What else? Misery loves company? Bingo...

It's all ok since *everyone* on Earth got irradiated

New Scientist reported on May 5, 2017, that scientists at the Norwegian Institute for Air Research had finished "the first global survey of radiation exposure caused by the meltdown" in Fukushima and had discovered that there was no need to worry. Why? Because the team "...calculated the approximate exposure of everyone on Earth to two radioactive isotopes of cesium, using all the data available so far."[242]

Geez... it's only an extra X-ray

Addressing the European Geosciences Union, the lead research scientist for the Norwegian Institute for Air Research announced that since "more than 80 % of the radiation was deposited in the ocean and poles... the global population got the least exposure... What I found was that we got one extra X-ray each..."[243] And while the team found that exposure to radiation in Japan was pretty low, except at Fukushima, "the effects on wildlife around the planet might be more severe. Already...increased levels of radiation around Fukushima have been linked to declines in bird populations there between 2011 and 2014 (and) 'there have also been reports of declines in other specie' such as insects and some mammals..."[244]

What a relief...

---

[242] newscientist.com/article/2129988-fukushima-accident-gave-everyone-an-x-rays-worth-of-radiation/

[243] newscientist.com/article/2129988-fukushima-accident-gave-everyone-an-x-rays-worth-of-radiation/

[244] newscientist.com/article/2129988-fukushima-accident-gave-everyone-an-x-rays-worth-of-radiation/

The lunch was really good
At the end of December 2018, a Japanese professor and career politician wrote an opinion piece in the Japan Times in which he downplayed radiation dangers at Fukushima.

The man reportedly recently toured the compound of Fukushima No.1, said that he never had to wear any protective gear, but acknowledged that it is "not yet completely safe" adding, though, the "lunch at the site was really good..."[245]

He then made this curious statement... "Fukushima's agricultural products have been declared safe after strict testing. In recent years we have bought and enjoyed rice, meat and vegetables cultivated in Fukushima. I was convinced that reputational risks abroad and import bans on those products are out of date and totally groundless."[246]

Oh. Ok... *Wait. What?*

Early warnings
Recipient of the Nobel Peace Prize, the group Physicians for Social Responsibility issued a statement in March 2011 which read in part, "Physicians for Social Responsibility (PSR) expressed concern over recent reports that radioactivity from the ongoing Fukushima accident is present in the Japanese food supply. While all food contains radionuclides, whether from natural

---

[245] japantimes.co.jp/opinion/2018/12/26/commentary/japan-commentary/busting-myths-fukushima-no-1/
[246] japantimes.co.jp/opinion/2018/12/26/commentary/japan-commentary/busting-myths-fukushima-no-1/

sources, nuclear testing or otherwise, the increased levels found in Japanese spinach and milk pose health risks to the population. PSR also expressed alarm over the level of misinformation circulating in press reports about the degree to which radiation exposure can be considered 'safe.'"

Yeah, but the dose is so small...
It's a matter of accumulation. The National Academy of Sciences stresses that "there are no safe doses of radiation. Decades of research show clearly that any dose of radiation increases an individual's risk for the development of cancer."[247] Any dose...

So to start calling an *All Clear* or to start chowing down on food grown in Fukushima should be a cautious step made after loads of testing and loads of corroboration...

Pass the milk...

---

[247] web.archive.org/web/20141112080628/https://www.psr.org/news-events/press-releases/psr-concerned-about-reports-increased-radioactivity-food-supply.html

RADIOACTIVE COWS

"There's nothing like sitting back and talking to your cows."

— Russell Crowe

When Fukushima happened, about 3,500 cattle on farms within 20 km of the nuclear plant were exposed to radiation.

About 2 months after the disaster in 2011, those cows were ordered to be killed, and not moved elsewhere, in order to keep people from eating them or selling them.

At the end of 2018 it was revealed by Japan Today that almost 430 of those cows had been secretly saved from slaughter by some local farmers. One farmer explained that he intended to protect his 50 cows to allow them to die naturally. While the radiation levels at his farm are a whopping 15-20 microsieverts per hour, a veterinarian who checks the cows claims all 50 cows are all perfectly healthy so far.[248]

So far...

---

[248] web.archive.org/web/20181227115859/https://japantoday.com/category/national/focus-farmers-struggle-to-keep-cows-left-behind-near-fukushima-plant

RADIOACTIVE WASTE

"At that time my notions of nuclear power were utterly idyllic. At school and at the university we had been taught that this was a magical factory that made 'energy out of nothing,' where people in white robes sat and pushed buttons. Chernobyl blew up when we were not prepared."

— Svetlana Alexievich

Six long years after the Fukushima meltdown, the waste was still piling up at staggering levels.

According to a report by Motoko Rich published in the New York Times on March 11, 2017, TEPCO was storing 962,000 tons of radioactive waste water in huge tanks in Fukushima while concurrently producing 400 tons of additional radioactive waste water *daily*. 400 tons! Daily! For a quick visual, think about adding 400 adult black rhinoceroses to your front yard, each and every day. Terrifying...

Apparently, the plan is to keep building more tanks... They also seem to have kicked around the idea of diluting some of the radioactive water and then simply releasing it into the ocean at "safe" levels, but local fishing businesses went berserk at the suggestion...

Piling it up

On top of the radioactive waste water, Fukushima reportedly had about "5,519 containers of radioactive sludge... 64,700 cubic meters of discarded protective clothing (the equivalent of 17 million one-gallon containers)... branches and logs from 220 acres of deforested land (80,000 cubic meters)... 200,400 cubic meters of radioactive rubble (from the explosions)... 3.5 billion gallons of soil (exposed to radiation)... (and) 1,573 nuclear fuel rods..."[249]

The distant atmosphere wasn't exempt either.

International reach

In December 2012, the Journal of Environmental Radioactivity revealed that Fukushima radionuclides (iodine-131, cesium-134 and 137 and plutonium-239 and 240) were discovered in many areas including Lithuania, Italy, France, Monaco, and the US. "The two maxima found in radionuclide concentrations were related to complicated long-range air mass transport from Japan across the Pacific, the North America and the Atlantic Ocean to Central Europe as indicated by modelling."[250]

Mud

In the meanwhile, apparently TEPCO had been sending and storing radioactive mud in many regions of Japan.

By 2019, Niigata prefecture and its people were fed up...

---

[249] nytimes.com/2017/03/11/world/asia/struggling-with-japans-nuclear-waste-six-years-after-disaster.html

[250] sciencedirect.com/science/article/pii/S0265931X11002992

On January 8, 2019, tired of having 60,000 tons of radioactive mud from the 2011 disaster stored in their prefecture about 200 km away from the Fukushima disaster, the "Niigata government said... it will ask (TEPCO) to shoulder the costs..." of finally removing it for good.[251] TEPCO reportedly had refused to handle "it saying it is not able to handle industrial waste... (but) TEPCO formally expressed its readiness to pay..."[252] *Whatever that means...*

Local officials had been storing the mud since they really didn't want to bury it on their lands even though it was claimed to be very low in radioactivity and "safe" for landfills.... "The contaminated mud, produced at an industrial water supply facility that takes in water from a river containing radioactive materials, is growing by 5,000 tons annually and the storage facility could become full later this year, according to the prefecture..."[253]

Endless...

---

[251] mainichi.jp/english/articles/20190108/p2g/00m/0dm/079000c

[252] mainichi.jp/english/articles/20190108/p2g/00m/0dm/079000c

[253] mainichi.jp/english/articles/20190108/p2g/00m/0dm/079000c

RADIOACTIVE POT

"Why use up the forests which were centuries in the making and the mines which required ages to lay down, if we can get the equivalent of forest and mineral products in the annual growth of the hemp fields?"

— Henry Ford

Just as so many politicians and communities are embracing cannabis again (George Washington and Thomas Jefferson both cultivated hemp for making clothes, Benjamin Franklin made parchment out of hemp, and the Declaration of Independence and the Constitution all were created on hemp paper),[254] Fukushima radiation may soon be embracing the growing hemp industry as well...

There are many online posts stating that hemp could be used to help clean up Fukushima.

In a process called *phytoremediation*, in which plants are used to draw toxins out of the water, soil, and air, industrial hemp (non-drug/low THC content) is being championed as a likely frontrunner.

Seriously.

---

[254] worldhistory.us/american-history/hemp-and-our-founding-fathers.php

Think about the possibilities...

Like a huge multi-tentacled vacuum cleaner, plants such as industrial hemp can scrub up a whole lot of badness... naturally... In fact, "phytoremediation can be used to remove radioactive elements from soil and water at former weapons producing facilities. It can also be used to clean up metals, pesticides, solvents, explosives, crude oil, polyaromatic hydrocarbons, and toxins leaching from landfills... Plants break down or degrade organic pollutants and stabilize metal contaminants by acting as filters or traps."[255]

Precedent exists

Way back in 1998, Central Oregon Green Pages reported that an Eastern European research scientist was leading the effort to clean up the Chernobyl nuclear disaster area and said that "Hemp is proving to be one of the best phytoremediative plants we have been able to find."[256] It seems that hemp actually thrives in some toxic soils, absorbing lead, nickel, and cadmium with no harm to itself...[257]

As reported by Fukushima Watch in 2015, "In the late 1990s, a group of representatives of Consolidated Growers and Processors used industrial hemp to help clean up a site near the Chernobyl disaster site..."[258]

---

[255] web.archive.org/web/20140110154417/https://www.hemp.net/news/9901/06/hemp_eats_chernobyl_waste.html

[256] web.archive.org/web/20140110154417/https://www.hemp.net/news/9901/06/hemp_eats_chernobyl_waste.html

[257] coloradopotguide.com/colorado-marijuana-blog/2015/september/11/radiation-disaster-hemp-can-help/

[258] fukushimawatch.com/2015-10-07-can-marijuana-save-the-fukushima-prefecture.html

In 2016 the town of Taranto, Italy, was using cannabis plants to help clean up toxic substances that had gotten into the soil and coming from a near-by steel plant, the largest in Europe.[259]

On the other hand...

Glowing stoners

Some of the world's most potent marijuana is grown in California. In March 2014, EnviroReporter's Michael Collins warned that Fukushima contamination had made it to the pot-growing soils of California. Apparently "two soil samples from near Willow Creek and from 'commercially available top soil in Northern California'" tested positive for Fukushima radiation.[260]

This development just begs for further testing in recreational-marijuana growing regions as well as an open investigation into the ramifications of any findings.

In the meantime, wouldn't it be cool if someone would just put together a catchy music video, complete with people dancing all over Fukushima, to prove everything is alright?

Enter possibly the most curious music video ever...

---

[259] slate.com/news-and-politics/2016/07/taranto-italy-is-decontaminating-its-land-by-cultivating-hemp.html

[260] enviroreporter.com/2014/03/fukushima-the-perfect-crime/all/1/

RADIOACTIVE VIDEOS

"It's ridiculous that time and time again we need a radioactive cloud coming out of a nuclear power-station to remind us that atomic energy is extraordinarily dangerous."

— Pierre Schaeffer

In Fukushima, there lives a best-selling author of books that show how to effectively use social media to grow business, who has also given TEDx talks, produces videos, and has trained people and lectured at companies such as Tokyo Mitsubishi UFJ Bank, SalesForce.com, Rahuten, various tourist agencies, and the prefectures of Fukushima, Niigata, and Fukui.[261]

She is also listed as Fukushima Prefecture's Official YouTube Channel Advisor. The official channel launched in November 2015 and seems to be called simply "Visit Fukushima."[262] It has over 22 million views and features videos promoting travel to Fukushima, with typical examples of travel, dining, drinking (sake), and sights to see.

---

[261] kumasakahitomi.com/profile

[262] youtube.com/channel/UCa6etLJzKLPTaaH2n_FW1ZA

On another YouTube Channel called PrefFukushima and touting that "We will be taking the viewers to the unchanging world of Fukushima's natural heritage we are so proud of.... which is famous in the world and has not changed..." she produced a video in 2016 showcasing the stories of three people who recently moved to Fukushima to create new lives and new futures...[263] Comments for this video were disabled.

Earlier, in 2014 she released a music video, "Happy Fukushima," on YouTube that she created to promote Fukushima. Japan Today reported that the video included snippets of "over 200 citizens of Fukushima from all walks of life dancing to (Pharrell) Williams' (megahit "Happy") song."[264] Daiji World reported that "the video shows students, Buddhist monks, cooks and executives dancing... in urban and natural settings of Fukushima" adding that "Around 50,000 residents from towns near the nuclear plant remain evacuated due to the radioactive emissions that have also seriously affected agriculture, livestock and local fish."[265]

Answering the obvious question, the creator insisted to the media that the video wasn't propaganda – that it was "100% independent" adding "No government, no TEPCO. I and my friends want people to know that we are also happy. That's all," she wrote.[266]

---

[263] youtube.com/watch?v=Gl6PZfqqEnc

[264] japantoday.com/category/features/lifestyle/residents-of-fukushima-really-are-this-happy

[265] daijiworld.com/news/newsDisplay.aspx?newsID=243138

[266] rt.com/news/164748-fukushima-happy-pharrell-williams/

In the video's description she clarifies that "Many people might think that Fukushima has been unhappy since 311 (March 11, 2011). But it's not true. With this video I want you to know that we are also happy and healthy just like you. Please enjoy our dance and share our happiness!"[267]

Yes, a scant three or so years after the Fukushima nuclear disaster began, a music video was filmed *entirely in Fukushima* to show the world everything is just fine and people in Fukushima are happy...

Strangely, the video is seemingly unavailable on US platforms so comments and reactions aren't obtainable to study. But Japan Today did note that **"not everyone can latch onto such an optimistic stance, especially with all the contradictory information circulating on the web, the mishandling of the situation by Tokyo Electric Power Company (TEPCO), and apparent cover-ups by the Japanese government. It's hard for anyone to know where the truth ends and the lies begin."[268]**

Again we turn to Japan Today that memorialized some of the alleged comments within their report stating that "'English-speaking foreigners online were quick to doubt the true happiness of people in Fukushima, as evidenced by the following YouTube comments:

- 'The people in Fukushima are happy? What in the world are they saying?'

---

[267] japantoday.com/category/features/lifestyle/residents-of-fukushima-really-are-this-happy

[268] japantoday.com/category/features/lifestyle/residents-of-fukushima-really-are-this-happy

- 'TEPCO's got everyone real good.'
- 'The people have been completely fooled by government propaganda.'
- "Why is no one coming out wearing a mask?"[269]

Maybe the most compelling was a comment *that wasn't a comment*. Someone on YouTube created a response video to "Happy Fukushima" featuring radiation readings from areas allegedly near those featured in the happy dancing scenes...

In this anti-happy video[270] apparently also shot in 2014 (versions of which keep disappearing from the web), scenes cut into the Happy Fukushima dance video show sands, debris, and dust strewn along the ground, near river beds, on children's play areas, bus stops, and more, all accompanied with meter readings showing radioactivity.

Before we proceed, a quick explanation from the Japan Atomic Energy Agency on radioactivity measured in microsieverts and potential dangers...

"...a range of radiation measured during normal hours in the past... roughly, it is usually in the order of 0.05 microsieverts per hour..." prior to the Fukushima disaster... "Now, there is a measurement point at which a value of 1.035 microsieverts per hour was recorded. ... if this value of 1.035 microsieverts per hour continued for a year, which is only an assumption, not a reality, the calculated

---

[269] japantoday.com/category/features/lifestyle/residents-of-fukushima-really-are-this-happy

[270] youtube.com/watch?v=BrLOlPwyWJc

cumulative radiation received for the one year time would be 9,066.6 microsieverts as a year consists of 8,760 hours... it is an amount of radiation a little smaller than that of the annual natural radiation at Guarapari, Brazil. It is a little more than one chest X-ray CT and one stomach X-ray examination each."[271]

Oh. Ok. So it sounds like the Japan Atomic Energy Agency is not too worried about readings of 1.035 microsieverts per hour since it's like 2 extra X-rays annually...

Seeing readings is believing
A YouTube channel describing itself as "Truth we must face...... !" features *hundreds* of videos of radioactivity readings from the Fukushima region and beyond.

Caveat: While we have no idea about the accuracy of the equipment used nor know anything about the man taking and posting the readings, he's been doing it since 2011 and has mostly favorable comments.

From what we could see, he launched with an April 2011 video in Oyama city, in Tochigi prefecture (about 100 miles from the disaster) and shows readings of over 0.8 microsieverts per hour taken at a street sewer drain.[272] A May 22, 2011 video from Iitate village, in Fukushima prefecture, shows a radiation reading of 6.78 microsieverts per hour.[273]

A selection of videotaped radiation readings from that one channel alone include:

---

[271] jaea.go.jp/english/jishin/kaisetsu01.pdf

[272] youtube.com/watch?v=nZXtH4JlMsM

[273] youtube.com/watch?v=kedC3Y5rmpU

- April 22, 2012, Kasumigajou Castle, Nihonmatsu city of Fukushima prefecture, radiation measured at 10.09 microsieverts per hour at ground level.[274]
- September 14, 2012, near Koriyama Daisan junior high school, Koriyama city, Fukushima prefecture (about 37 miles from the disaster), a radioactivity reading of 16.07 microsieverts per hour was recorded in street dust amidst high school students running around.[275]
- September 30, 2012, SEKIYA elementary school of Nasushiobara city, Tochigi prefecture, about 75 miles from the disaster, with various radiation readings including 8.1 microsieverts per hour from dust on grass.[276]
- November 24, 2012, Tshushima junior High School, Namie, Fukushima prefecture, various radiation readings including 12.21 microsieverts per hour on the ground.[277]
- November 24, 2012, fallen leaves near Ukedo river bridge, Namie, Fukushima Prefecture, measured at 42.33 microsieverts per hour.[278]
- January 20, 2013, on a road in front of Kashiwa high school, Kashiwa city, Chiba prefecture, (about 124 miles from the disaster but 21 miles from the center of Tokyo), radioactive readings were at 1.41 microsieverts per hour.[279]

---

[274] youtube.com/watch?v=E0vaLDzT4po

[275] youtube.com/watch?v=t7I-2QM3UuM

[276] youtube.com/watch?v=FbD0IajnBhM

[277] youtube.com/watch?v=KAWmyxkW3TE

[278] youtube.com/watch?v=JS8_9S-OeqQ

[279] youtube.com/watch?v=dwiHR91Q2Go

- April 5, 2013, dust from the side of a road in Namie, Fukushima prefecture (about 6 miles from the disaster) measured in at 86.09 microsieverts per hour.[280]
- October 12, 2013, radiation of 7.08 microsieverts per hour was detected in mud near a bicycle parking lot near official Fukushima Prefecture Government offices in Fukushima City.[281]
- November 30, 2013 (Two years and eight months since the nuclear power plant accident) mud on the riverbank of Abukuma River, Watari, Fukushima City, Fukushima Prefecture was measured at 9.99 microsieverts per hour.[282]
- November 30, 2013, parking lot pavement in front of NHK Fukushima broadcasting station, in Koriyama, Fukushima prefecture (about 37 miles from the disaster) a radioactivity reading of 7.24 microsieverts per hour was recorded.[283]
- April 26, 2014, 113 microsieverts per hour were detected in dust on a road near a temple in Namie, Fukushima prefecture, about 6 miles from the disaster.[284]
- November 23, 2014, 2.0 microsieverts per hour were detected at the Kashiwa campus at Tokyo University in moss by the tennis courts.[285]
- November 3, 2014, at a rest area in the northern part of Nihonmatsu city, Fukushima prefecture,

[280] youtube.com/watch?v=M4mruK5UxRY

[281] youtube.com/watch?v=nPKXecV7Q08

[282] youtube.com/watch?v=AQo3wf3A34I

[283] youtube.com/watch?v=8V2VnRDv33E

[284] youtube.com/watch?v=IuVJOc1q6mw

[285] youtube.com/watch?v=irxojLLULs4

between the grass and asphalt paving, 4 - 5 microsieverts per hour were detected.[286]

- October 24, 2015, 22 microsieverts per hour were detected about 6 miles away from the disaster in sand and fallen leaves near a temple in Namie town of Fukushima prefecture.[287]
- November 7, 2015, radiation measurements in the air on the hiking trails of Mt. Ryozen in Date city, Fukushima prefecture, measured 0.4–0.9 microsieverts per hour.[288]
- April 2, 2016, radiation in mud around Gohyaku-gara river, Motomiya city, Fukushima prefecture, was recorded at 9-10 microsieverts per hour.[289]
- July 16, 2016, Gohyakubuchi-park of Koriyama city, Fukushima Prefecture, yielded a radiation reading of 1.55 microsieverts per hour in the woods.[290]
- March 18, 2017 (6 years after the nuclear disaster), at the "Wild Bird Forest" at Gohyakubuchi-park of Koriyama city, Fukushima Prefecture, up to 1.34 microsieverts per hour were detected by a meter held in the air about chest-height.[291]
- April 22, 2017, radiation in front of a temple, Namie town of Fukushima prefecture came in at 18-20 microsieverts per hour when meter was placed on the soil.[292]

---

[286] youtube.com/watch?v=nn-5zvCVJMc

[287] youtube.com/watch?v=VshJFhxrBNs

[288] youtube.com/watch?v=LRp0lsTNulY

[289] youtube.com/watch?v=feHeZHb7toY

[290] youtube.com/watch?v=3zx7BCQ7OW0

[291] youtube.com/watch?v=SFcbMPM7454

[292] youtube.com/watch?v=Uz-YZr2gl6w

- June 10, 2017, a meter placed on the ground near a park entrance at Bentenyama park in Fukushima city, Fukushima prefecture, it yielded a radiation reading of 3.5-3.7 microsieverts per hour. [293]

At a minimum, these readings don't make you think *everything is ok...*

Strange how the story of Fukushima and its prospects to recover seem to depend heavily upon the perspective and motives of the storytellers.

If only a comic book hero could fix everything.

---

[293] youtube.com/watch?v=usqVoXKcEUl

RADIOACTIVE COMICS

"From history and teenage romance to futuristic science fiction and profound themes of life, manga became an important, almost inevitable aspect of Japan's identity and they helped spread knowledge and understanding of it across the planet.."

— Angie Kordic, Lorenzo Pereira, Elena Martinique

The Japanese passion for comics, known as "manga," knows no bounds. People of all ages routinely escape reality and pass some free time indulging in manga.

As noted in a Widewalls editorial, "With a long history deeply rooted in the rich Japanese art, manga are one of the most fascinating phenomena in Japan and the whole world... these comics have been a major player in the country's publishing industry, creating a robust market, reaching millions of readers of all ages..."[294]

Pretty powerful stuff... no doubt with the power to sway.

Enter the popular *Oishinbo* manga series.

Published since 1983, Oishinbo means "The Gourmet" and is about a pair of fictional food journalists in search

---

[294] widewalls.ch/japanese-manga-comics-history/

of gourmet food. High drama and mature themes meld to create engrossing tales. The question is, did some subject matter come too close to the truth? Or was it simply capitalizing on spreading fear?

Nose bleeds

In April and May 2014, a "new chapter of Oishinbo sees its protagonist returning from a brief trip to Fukushima, whereupon he suddenly begins to experience nosebleeds... a bespectacled man... then arrives on the scene to explain that he, too, has been suffering with nosebleeds since the accident at the Fukushima Daiichi Nuclear Power Plant in 2011..."[295]

You should know that in the comic this "bespectacled man" bears a strong visual resemblance to a retired mayor of a town in Fukushima. More on that later.

Addressing the fictional gourmet food journalists, the bespectacled character reveals that "In Fukushima, there are a lot of people who suffer from the same symptoms. They just don't talk about it..."[296]

Later, to make sure his message is crystal clear, the character proclaims that "people should not live in Fukushima today."[297]

Those are some pretty strong words.

---

[295] soranews24.com/2014/05/16/nosebleeds-food-and-fear-how-a-popular-manga-became-the-centre-of-a-debate-about-fukushima/
[296] soranews24.com/2014/05/16/nosebleeds-food-and-fear-how-a-popular-manga-became-the-centre-of-a-debate-about-fukushima/
[297] soranews24.com/2014/05/16/nosebleeds-food-and-fear-how-a-popular-manga-became-the-centre-of-a-debate-about-fukushima/

But that ominous character wasn't done.

Using specific locations and examples, the bespectacled character "alludes to a survey conducted in Osaka, where a large amount of rubble taken from Northeast Japan was shipped during the post-tsunami clean-up operation. He states that 800 out of 1,000 people living close to the site where this rubble is being kept reported having nosebleeds and feeling generally ill."[298]

The resulting public turmoil was huge.

The retired mayor of a town in Fukushima, *who looks surprisingly similar to the drawings of the "bespectacled man,"* posted pictures of his bespectacled self with nosebleeds on his Facebook page.

In the meanwhile, the writer of the comic said his inspiration was simply from his own experiences with nosebleeds after a trip to Fukushima.

As you might expect by now, the government went into overdrive to assure people that *although radiation exposure can cause nosebleeds,* the radioactivity outside the no-go zones wouldn't be high enough to cause the bleeding.

Authorities responded to the rubble featured in the comic by stating that the rubble was real but "in no way posed a health risk to residents."[299]

---

[298] soranews24.com/2014/05/16/nosebleeds-food-and-fear-how-a-popular-manga-became-the-centre-of-a-debate-about-fukushima/

[299] soranews24.com/2014/05/16/nosebleeds-food-and-fear-how-a-popular-manga-became-the-centre-of-a-debate-about-fukushima/

Hurt feelings and lost money

The Fukushima prefecture government issued a statement stating that "'the feelings of the Fukushima people were totally ignored and deeply hurt.' The prefecture's economy and tourism industry, too, it added, would likely suffer as a result of the statements made in the comic, despite the fact that 'it has been made clear through the appraisal of experts that there is no causal relationship between radiation exposure among residents and nosebleeds.'"[300]

Who knows what the truth is at this point...

Clearly, resettling abandoned areas would change the optics still plaguing Fukushima... but at what cost?

---

[300] soranews24.com/2014/05/16/nosebleeds-food-and-fear-how-a-popular-manga-became-the-centre-of-a-debate-about-fukushima/

RADIOACTIVE REPOPULATION

<blockquote>

""If there is anything the nuclear industry learned from Chernobyl, it's that a large exclusion zone is bad for business. It's a constant reminder that a nuclear disaster is irreversible, and it's women and children who are bearing the brunt."

— Kendra Ulrich
Senior Global Energy Campaigner
Greenpeace Japan.

</blockquote>

In 2015 evacuation orders in certain areas started to be lifted and people were encouraged to return to the homes they had abandoned.

Just the beginning

In one case, a town's mayor said" the lifting of the order was only the starting line for reconstruction. The finish line, he said, was an environment where the people could live peacefully and be 'rich of mind,' thus showing his determination to build a new town together with its citizens..."[301]

Not surprisingly, many people weren't too eager to go back to the former no-go zones.

---

[301] jaif.or.jp/en/lifting-of-evacuation-order-for-naraha-town-marks-step-forward-toward-reconstruction-of-fukushima/

In 2015, DW revealed that it appeared that the Japanese government was attempting to speed up repopulation of areas around Fukushima even as "environmentalists say many areas still show highly-elevated levels of contamination and are unfit for habitation..."[302]

Normalizing radiation?

Greenpeace accused Japan of attempting to "'normalize' a nuclear disaster. If the public can be convinced that less than five years after the worst nuclear disaster in a generation, citizens can go home and return to life the way it was before the disaster – with no additional health risks – then that is a powerful argument against the majority of Japanese citizens who oppose nuclear reactor restarts..."[303]

In limbo

In 2015 while summarizing their position on Fukushima repopulation efforts, Greenpeace held no punches and concluded that "to keep the victims of the Fukushima Daiichi nuclear disaster in limbo, many crammed into tiny temporary housing cubicles, for nearly five years is inhumane. To force these citizens back into such heavily contaminated areas via the economic leverage the Government holds over them is a gross iniquity. And for the International Atomic Energy Agency to assist the Japanese Government in the propaganda war being waged on Fukushima victims not only undermines whatever credibility it may have, but

---

[302] dw.com/en/tokyo-under-fire-for-plans-to-speed-return-of-fukushima-evacuees/a-18597707

[303] greenpeace.org/archive-international/en/news/Blogs/nuclear-reaction/Fukushima-nuclear-victims-forced-resettlement-litate/blog/53584/

amounts to it being an accomplice in a crime against the people of Japan…"[304]

Just own up…
One Fukushima survivor testified in 2017 to the United Nations about human rights abuses she claims Fukushima residents suffered because the Japanese government and TEPCO "won't admit their responsibilities."[305]

Financial pressure
In 2017, DW reported that evacuees of the Fukushima disaster were being pressured to return to an area that Greenpeace said still exceeded international guidelines for radiation safety… "according to environmental organization Greenpeace, it's uncertain whether many will want to. Greenpeace says tests it has carried out on homes in Iitate show that despite decontamination, radiation levels are still dangerously high - but that's not stopping the Japanese government from pressuring evacuees from returning, under threat of losing financial support."[306]

Radiation levels unacceptable at a nuclear plant
Maybe the most powerful example used by Greenpeace to get their safety point across was the fact that "If these radiation levels were measured in a nuclear facility… prompt action would be required by the authorities to mitigate serious adverse consequences for human

[304] greenpeace.org/archive-international/en/news/Blogs/nuclear-reaction/Fukushima-nuclear-victims-forced-resettlement-Iitate/blog/53584/
[305] greenpeace.org/archive-international/en/press/releases/2017/Fukushima-survivor-submits-evidence-to-UN-over-Japanese-government-human-rights-abuses-/
[306] dw.com/en/fukushima-nuclear-disaster-evacuees-pressured-to-return-to-contaminated-homes-says-greenpeace/a-37639353

health and safety, property or the environment."[307] So people are being told to return to an area that radioactively measures so high that a similar measurement inside a working nuclear facility would trigger a serious health and safety response.

Nasty stuff.

Meet Baskut Tuncak

Tuncak is the UN Special Rapporteur and expert on the implications for human rights of the environmentally sound management and disposal of hazardous substances and wastes.

On October 25, 2018, Tuncak was featured in a UN press release from the Office of the High Commissioner/Human Rights.[308] Seems Tuncak found that "the Japanese Government's decision to raise by 20 times what it considered to be an acceptable level of radiation exposure was deeply troubling, highlighting in particular the potentially grave impact of excessive radiation on the health and wellbeing of children..."[309]

Yes. You read that right.

If you can't meet the standard, change it...

Following the 2011 Fukushima disaster the Japanese Government "raised the acceptable level of radiation for

---

[307] dw.com/en/fukushima-nuclear-disaster-evacuees-pressured-to-return-to-contaminated-homes-says-greenpeace/a-37639353

[308] ohchr.org/EN/NewsEvents/Pages/DisplayNews.aspx?NewsID=23772&LangID=E

[309] ohchr.org/EN/NewsEvents/Pages/DisplayNews.aspx?NewsID=23772&LangID=E

residents in Fukushima from 1 mSv/year to 20 mSv/year…"[310]

Kind of like, well, there ain't no way we're gonna see "1" any time soon so, presto, now "20" is safe…

In 2017, the UN human rights monitoring mechanism recommended that Japan lower the acceptable radiation level back to 1 mSv/year and according to the UN, Japan agreed, but according to Tuncak, Japan did nothing to lower its levels to that safer range.

Save the children
Member countries of the "UN Convention on the Rights of the Child, to which Japan is a Party, contains a clear obligation on States to respect, protect and fulfil the right of the child to life, to maximum development and to the highest attainable standard of health, taking their best interests into account. This, the expert (Tuncak) said, requires State parties such as Japan to prevent and minimize avoidable exposure to radiation and other hazardous substances." Obviously. Part of keeping children safe and healthy is to keep them away, far away, from radioactive waste. *Duh…*

So what's the big deal? Let's go over it again. And then add in the *glowing* curve ball…

Japan has their official acceptable level of radiation pegged at 1 millisievert per year. *Fukushima happens.* Japan increases the official acceptable level by 1,900%

---

[310] ohchr.org/EN/NewsEvents/Pages/DisplayNews.aspx?NewsID=23772&LangID=E

to a whopping 20 millisieverts per year... (20 millisieverts = 20,000 microsieverts.)

According to the UN Commission, a "dose of 20 millisieverts per year is only acceptable for 'occupational' exposure... where someone has taken a job in a place where radioactive exposures are unavoidable."

In fact, since 1985, the International Commission on Radiological Protection has "recommended that any public be exposed to no more than a 1 millisievert dose per year."[311]

Here comes that *glowing* curve ball...

Seems Japan was *relocating* "evacuees who are children and women of reproductive age to areas of Fukushima where radiation levels remain higher than what was considered safe or healthy before the nuclear disaster seven years ago."[312]

No wonder Tuncak blew a fuse!

Pressure on top of pressure
Tuncak felt that "the combination of the Government's decision to lift evacuation orders and the prefectural authorities' decision to cease the provision of housing subsidies, places a large number of self-evacuees under immense pressure to return... The gradual lifting of evacuation orders has created enormous strains on

---

[311] qz.com/1439696/families-are-returning-to-fukushima-and-japan-may-be-violating-their-human-rights-says-the-un/

[312] ohchr.org/EN/NewsEvents/Pages/DisplayNews.aspx?NewsID=23772&LangID=E

people whose lives have already been affected by the worst nuclear disaster of this century. Many feel they are being forced to return to areas that are unsafe, including those with radiation levels above what the Government previously considered safe."[313]

Going public
Calling Japan on the carpet, Tuncak said this and more of the same in a presentation to the UN General Assembly in New York City on October 25, 2018.

Japanese delegates were not pleased. Not at all...

Too eager
The Nikkei Asian Review correctly reported that Tuncak "criticized the Japanese government... as too eager to send Fukushima Prefecture residents back to the homes from which well over 100,000 were displaced by the March 2011 earthquake, tsunami and nuclear disaster."

A Japanese delegation representative responded by expressing "strong opposition" to Tuncak's report and took shots at the "accuracy of Tuncak's current and past news releases. "[314]

Facts propagate negativity?
The Japanese delegation representative also charged that "Tuncak's news release invites inaccurate media reports and propagates Fukushima's negative reputation..." even as "Japan is making efforts with a

---

[313] ohchr.org/EN/NewsEvents/Pages/DisplayNews.aspx?NewsID=23772&LangID=E

[314] asia.nikkei.com/Politics/Japan-should-not-push-residents-back-to-Fukushima-UN-expert

view to 'dissipating this negative reputation and restoring life back to normal.'"[315]

Unwavering, Tuncak stood by his view of the facts.

Still wary after all these years

On January 16, 2019, *Scientific American* ran an article on Fukushima. Some 122,0000 people had been cleared to return. The subhead said it all "Eight years after the nuclear meltdown, wary citizens are moving back to contaminated homesteads—some not by choice."

Very interestingly, *Scientific American* noted that Japan's "Prime Minister Shinzo Abe is determined to end all evacuations by 2020, when Japan will host the Olympic Summer Games. The events will include baseball and softball competitions in Fukushima City, a mere 55 miles from the ruined reactors..."[316]

Now hold on there. That could explain a lot...

---

[315] asia.nikkei.com/Politics/Japan-should-not-push-residents-back-to-Fukushima-UN-expert

[316] scientificamerican.com/article/fukushima-residents-return-despite-radiation/

RADIOACTIVE OLYMPICS?

"Holding an Olympic Games means evoking history."

— Pierre de Coubertin
Founder
International Olympic Committee

In 2013, Tokyo knocked out Istanbul and Madrid and won the bid to host the 2020 Summer Olympics. The Japanese vowed to deliver "well-organized and safe Games that will reinforce the Olympic values while demonstrating the benefits of sport to a new generation."[317]

This will be 2nd time in history that Japan will host summer games. They hosted the "Summer Games of 1964, which were the first to be staged in Asia."[318] As The New York Times noted, "Back then, the Olympics symbolized Japan's recovery from World War II; similarly, organizers in Japan had seen the 2020 Games as a chance to show the world that their country was bouncing back from the devastating March 2011 tsunami and the nuclear disaster at Fukushima."[319]

---

[317] olympic.org/tokyo-2020

[318] olympic.org/tokyo-2020

[319] nytimes.com/2019/01/11/world/europe/japan-olympics-corruption-tsunekazu-takeda.html

Those 1964 games "radically transformed the country," and the 2020 Games are a vitally important national event with the Japanese organizers claiming the Games will be "the most innovative ever organized, and will rest on three fundamental principles to transform the world: striving for your personal best (achieving your personal best); accepting one another (unity in diversity); and passing on a legacy for the future (connecting to tomorrow)."[320]

No room for *any* disruptions. None! No matter what...

Promoting Fukushima
At some point, the president of the International Olympic Committee (IOC) apparently got the notion or inspiration from somewhere that holding part of the Olympic games physically in the Fukushima area would be a great thing to do...

By March 2017, about six short years after the disaster started, the IOC proudly announced that it had approved the Azuma Stadium *in Fukushima prefecture* to hold Olympic softball and baseball matches.

EcoWatch reported in July 2017 that the IOC "is working overtime to normalize the situation... even though conditions at Fukushima are anything but normal. The commission even has plans for the 2020 Tokyo Olympics to have baseball and softball games played at Fukushima."[321] At the time, the IOC president also said at a press conference that "This is a great opportunity to bring the spirit of the Olympic Games to

---

[320] olympic.org/tokyo-2020

[321] ecowatch.com/tokyo-olympics-fukushima-2460798164.html

this region, which was affected by the tsunami in 2011," and that "It is also an expression of solidarity of the Olympic Movement with the people in this region who are suffering from the consequences of this disaster. We are really happy that we could approve this, following the discussions I had during my last visit to Japan with Prime Minister Abe..."[322]

The Olympics are coming, straighten up your room!

Bye-bye Sun Child
In October 2018 the Japan Atomic Industrial Forum reported that Fukushima was removing its statue of the "Sun Child." Towering about 20 feet into the air, the somewhat creepy statue, sporting anime-themed eyes, depicts what appears to be a boy in a yellow hazmat suit, having removed his helmet which he's holding in one hand, a model of the sun held in his other hand, some sort of bandage on his cheek, and wearing a chest-level nuclear radiation meter that reads "000." It was apparently meant to joyously signify that all the radiation in Fukushima is now gone, and it's safe to remove your protective helmets.

Apparently after some criticism about "giving bad impressions," sending an "uncomfortable message" and "stoking fear"[323] the statue was slated to be removed, even though as one writer noted, "It is not clear if any of those views represent a majority of public opinion. Indeed, many people in the prefecture... personally wanted the piece to remain. In the end, the decision was

---

[322] olympic.org/news/fukushima-to-host-baseball-and-softball-matches-at-the-olympic-games-tokyo-2020
[323] jaif.or.jp/en/the-implications-of-removing-the-sun-child-statue-in-fukushima/

that it had to go as long as it hurt some residents' feelings."

Oh. Ok. So a few people have hurt feelings and everyone goes along? Really?

Radioactive selfies

Actually, we're thinking it was really more about the 2020 Olympics. If you're trying to reinvent yourself, the *last* thing you need in the middle of town, and sure to be discovered by foreign media as well as tourists and Olympians looking for selfie photo ops, is an enormous freaky statue that screams <<RADIATION>> word of which would spread faster than an atom splitting on the plains of social media...

Bye-bye swastikas

Today, the swastika in Japan is not used to honor Japan's World War II alliance with Adolf Hitler and Nazi Germany. Called a "manji," the swastika is actually a good luck symbol in Japan and most often associated with Buddhist temples – although it dates back thousands of years and is linked to many ancient cultures. (The oldest known carving of swastikas is 15,000 years old and found in the Ukraine.[324])

The challenge was that the Japanese use the swastika pictograph on maps and signs to represent the location of Buddhist temples... In preparation for the 2020 Olympics, as the BBC reported in January 2016, "Despite the swastika's origins in the ancient language of Sanskrit and its centuries-old association with

---

[324]bbc.com/news/magazine-29644591

Japanese Buddhism, the GSI found that many tourists still associated it with the Nazis…" therefore Japan will "drop the use of the swastika and other confusing symbols on maps for foreign tourists following complaints that they are offensive or hard to understand…"[325]

At the same time, the BBC noted that there were no reported corresponding plans to force Buddhist temples to remove their ancient swastika symbols for 2020.

Bye-bye porn mags

On January 22, 2019, The Mainichi reported that "Japan's top three convenience store chain operators… have decided to stop selling adult magazines nationwide by the end of August to improve their image ahead of the Rugby World Cup this fall and Tokyo Olympics and Paralympics next year."[326]

Hello Olympic torches

On January 1, 2019, it was announced that "recycled aluminum from temporary housing in Fukushima… is planned to be used in the crafting of Tokyo 2020 Olympic torches."[327] Very touching.

Yet, amidst preparations for the 2020 Olympics, some are focused on something more disconcerting than statues, swastikas, and porn… Remember Arnie Gundersen? The nuclear industry expert, veteran of 70 US atomic energy

---

[325] theguardian.com/world/2016/jan/20/japan-to-drop-the-swastika-from-its-tourist-maps

[326] mainichi.jp/english/articles/20190122/p2g/00m/0dm/036000c#cxrecs_s

[327] mainichi.jp/english/articles/20190101/p2g/00m/0sp/048000c

projects, and licensed nuclear reactor operator with 45 years of experience? He's back and he's super concerned...

Possible motive behind the rush

Commenting specifically on the 2020 Summer Olympics to EcoWatch, Gundersen said the nuclear energy industry and the government of Japan are "trying to force almost all of the people who evacuated their homes in the wake of the Fukushima nuclear disaster to return 'home' before the 2020 Tokyo Olympics..."[328] Gundersen warned that "The disaster is not 'over' and 'home' no longer is habitable."[329]

Never go back

Instead of nuances and carefully scripted tripe, Gundersen further explained what is likely *really* going on behind the scenes – "Big banks and large electric utilities and energy companies are putting profit before public health... Luckily, my two young grandsons live in the U.S.; if their parents lived instead in Fukushima, I would tell them to leave and never go back."[330]

Gundersen added that "Holding the 2020 Olympics in Japan is an effort by the current Japanese government to make these ongoing atomic reactor meltdowns disappear from the public eye."[331]

At what safety level?

Here's a very simple question... Will all the areas where Olympic events are to be held be at safe radiation

---

[328] ecowatch.com/tokyo-olympics-fukushima-2460798164.html

[329] ecowatch.com/tokyo-olympics-fukushima-2460798164.html

[330] ecowatch.com/tokyo-olympics-fukushima-2460798164.html

[331] ecowatch.com/tokyo-olympics-fukushima-2460798164.html

levels? And not the "new" higher levels, but the 1 millisievert per year UN level? Remember that in 2017, the United Nations human rights monitoring mechanism recommended that Japan lower the level back to 1 millisievert and according to the UN, Japan agreed, but according to the UN Special Rapporteur Tuncak, Japan did *nothing* to lower its levels to that safer range? Is that still the case? How would you really know? *And how might a higher level affect people attending the 2020 Olympics? Fair question?*

At what risk?
Will people be warned so they can make informed choices, or will there be no attempt? Seriously, who would go to the 2020 Olympics without knowing the risks, if any? Even if just for your own piece of mind...

Towering tsunami. Major carnage. Bad-ass nuclear meltdown. Radioactive waste. Big banks. Dominant utilities. Powerful government officials. Profit before people. This has all the trappings of some sort of Hollywood movie about a futuristic dystopian affair. Except for bribery and fraud, it seems all there...

Olympic prestige
In the meanwhile, to host the Olympics in Japan sure is an impressive public relations move. And to have Olympic athletes compete in Fukushima – wow – epic! Scenes of summer baseball being played and happy Olympians eating and frolicking all over Fukushima sure would go a long way in repairing Fukushima's reputation, economy, and spirit...

No wonder the government and the nuclear authorities all seem so eager to get Fukushima all squared away...

Wow. Makes you really appreciate what a stroke of luck it was that Japan won the 2020 Summer Games bid at this exact place in time...

Luck? *Maybe.* Maybe not.

Bribery claims
On January 11, 2019, it was reported in The New York Times that Japan's Olympic Committee president had been "indicted on corruption charges in France after an investigation into the bidding process that led to Tokyo's being awarded the Summer Games it is preparing to host next year."[332]

African connection
The French prosecutors claim that bribes were paid to "African Olympic committee officials for their votes..." and contend that another African, the former president of the International Association of Athletics Federations, was involved in the bribery scheme, and is also suspected in "facilitating and accepting bribes from officials behind Rio de Janeiro's successful bid to host the 2016 Summer Olympics..."[333]

According to the Los Angeles Times, "At issue are approximately $2 million in payments reportedly made to a Singapore-based consultant around the time of the 2013 host-city vote..."[334]

---

[332] nytimes.com/2019/01/11/world/europe/japan-olympics-corruption-tsunekazu-takeda.html

[333] nytimes.com/2019/01/11/world/europe/japan-olympics-corruption-tsunekazu-takeda.html

[334] latimes.com/sports/olympics/la-sp-tokyo-corruption-20190111-story.html

Of course, all of this is completely unrelated and just another unfortunate coincidence...

And, of course, everyone is innocent – until they confess or are proven guilty...

It will be very interesting to see how many people will actually show up in Fukushima for that part of the Summer Olympic Games. Betting Arnie Gundersen and Dr. Helen Caldicott won't be in the stands...

Something to seriously ponder
If you had literally everything riding on a good positive strong showing at the 2020 Olympics, both nationally, as well as for the reinvention and reinvigoration of Fukushima, how far would you be willing to push the envelope, if at all?

Would you be able to look the other way if you knew radiation levels here and there were high? After all, visitors might not be exposed to all that much, right?

They're only coming in for the Olympics and then leaving, right? And doesn't it take quite a bit of time for bad stuff to happen health-wise? And nothing may happen anyway, correct?

Fukushima could really *really* use this event to recoup years of economic and agricultural malaise, right? Aren't the upsides for Fukushima just overwhelmingly positive? And is the only downside maybe a little bit of extra radiation for unsuspecting or uninformed masses?

Oh man! That's got to be a hard choice to have to make...

RADIOACTIVE AFTERWORD

> "Young people with families—they don't believe the
> government radiation measurements."
>
> — Shuzo Sasaki

Even as it bravely rebuilds and reinvents itself,
Fukushima is in a world of hurt.

On one hand, the local people desperately want to
return to their pre-nuclear-disaster lives. It was tragic
enough that so many thousands died and so much
property was destroyed in the tsunami devastation. Yet,
with no time to grieve or think or anything, the nuclear
disaster followed on the heels of the deadly waves
causing additional untold tragedy.

So, yes, the people of Fukushima want to recover. They
want their businesses to thrive and their agriculture to
be plentiful. They want their families to be healthy.
They want to be happy.

On the other hand, the authorities and the power
company appear to want to get the disaster behind
them as soon as possible. Thousands of displaced
people and swarms of cleanup crews in the region are a
constant *unwelcome* reminder that things aren't "back
to normal" yet.

With the 2020 Olympics coming to town very soon, it provides the motive for hurriedly and aggressively resettling previously evacuated areas and finishing high visibility cleanups. And the radioactive particles, whether in tanks, or in black disposal bags, in storm drains, on river banks, in forests, or lying on the ground, remain a constant source of worry.

Can the goals of the people mesh with the goals of the authorities? And result in a safe, healthy, and wealthy outcome for all? We sincerely hope so…

Here's the deadly rub
You can't see, smell, hear, or taste radioactive elements. Not in your air. Not in your water. Not in your food. No warnings without meter readings or lab testing. And radiation exposure, unless the levels are very high, usually doesn't result in instant death. And levels can be cumulative and build up silently over years.

While no level of radiation is healthy, will everyone exposed to radiation develop health issues? Of course not.

Will the *levels* of radioactivity and your *length of exposure* matter? For sure. But it can still take years for health issues to manifest.

It's literally a waiting game.

So to push through clean up campaigns and to hurriedly resettle areas while still trying to effectively address a major nuclear disaster seems as though it could very likely create its own new set of troubling issues.

WHO knew

The World Health Organization (WHO) specifically named cancer as a possible consequence of the Fukushima nuclear disaster. More specifically, "a study published in 2015 in the scientific journal Epidemiology suggested that children who were exposed to radiation in Fukushima at the time of the meltdown were likely to develop thyroid cancer more frequently."[335]

Loads of "unrelated" thyroid cancer?

In June 2017, authorities announced a running total of 152 cases of thyroid cancer among people who lived in Fukushima during the disaster. But just to be clear, "the prefectural government... has remained adamant that the cancer cases were not directly linked to the nuclear accident and ensuing radiation."[336]

Dutifully, the physician who heads a committee in Fukushima screening for thyroid cancer in adolescents told the press, ""It's hard to think there is any relationship"[337] with radiation...

Seriously? Hard to think?

Denial in the face of a paid bill?

Just one example of denial. According to a March 31, 2017 report in the International Business Times, "The Fukushima Medical University, run by the prefectural government... denied that any child under the age of

---

[335] ibtimes.com/fukushima-nuclear-radiation-causing-more-cases-thyroid-cancer-2549543

[336] ibtimes.com/fukushima-nuclear-radiation-causing-more-cases-thyroid-cancer-2549543

[337] ibtimes.com/fukushima-nuclear-radiation-causing-more-cases-thyroid-cancer-2549543

five had developed thyroid cancer.... However, an audit of medical receipts conducted by the 3.11 Children's Fund for Thyroid Cancer, who paid the 4-year-old boy's medical bills, found that he had an operation at the facility to remove his thyroid gland."[338]

If you want to understand how deep denial goes, reread the last paragraph slowly. It's all there...

TEPCO executives indicted
In late December 2018, we learned that 3 top TEPCO executives were "charged with professional negligence resulting in death and injury over the March 2011 nuclear accident... they are accused of neglecting to take preventive measures while being aware that a massive tsunami could cause an accident at the plant, forcing patients at Futaba Hospital in the Fukushima Prefecture town of Okuma to take shelter for a long time and causing 44 of them to die."[339] The defendants are each facing a potential of 5 years in prison if convicted.

TEPCO is facing lawsuits from survivors and families of victims of the disaster. By October 2017, 10,000+ "people joined the roughly 30 suits filed at courts across the country."[340] Expect those numbers to grow.

Finally, an acknowledgment, albeit posthumously
In 2018, a man in his 50s who worked for TEPCO for over 30 years, mostly at the Fukushima nuclear plant, died of lung cancer which had been diagnosed in 2016.

---

[338] ibtimes.com/fukushima-nuclear-radiation-caused-thyroid-cancer-4-year-old-2518750
[339] mainichi.jp/english/articles/20181226/p2a/00m/0na/032000c
[340] japantimes.co.jp/news/2017/10/10/national/crime-legal/court-orders-tepco-government-pay-damages-fukushima-disaster/#.XEfN-IVKiUl

Among his duties were "measuring radiation levels at the plant and its premises immediately after the incident."[341]

His death was the first officially acknowledged by Japan as having been a direct consequence of exposure to radiation from the Fukushima disaster.

According to The New York Times, the Japanese government reported that the man "had been exposed to a lifetime dose of 195 millisieverts of radiation after working at Fukushima and other plants... Safety regulators say workers can be safely exposed to up to 50 millisieverts a year, but if a worker with an accumulated 100 millisieverts develops an illness after five years of exposure, that can be ruled an occupational injury." An expert was cited as saying that "the man had been exposed to 74 millisieverts at the Fukushima plant since the accident."[342]

Japan has also officially recognized that another 4 TEPCO workers "all still surviving, have developed leukemia or thyroid cancer that the government recognizes as being caused by exposure during their work at Fukushima Daiichi."[343]

Acknowledgement is a step in the right direction.

Sadly, this is likely just the beginning of many more acknowledgments...

---

[341] rt.com/news/437711-fukushima-radiation-exposure-death/
[342] nytimes.com/2018/09/05/world/asia/japan-fukushima-radiation-cancer-death.html
[343] soranews24.com/2018/09/06/first-worker-to-die-from-fukushima-radiation-exposure-officially-recognized-by-japans-government/